DOUGLAS ADAMS was born in 1952 and created all the contradictory manifestations of *The Hitchhiker's Guide to the Galaxy*: radio, novels, TV, computer game, stage adaptation, comic book and towel. He lectured and broadcast round the world and was a patron of the Dian Fossey Gorilla Fund and Save the Rhino International. Douglas lived with his wife Jane and daughter Polly in Islington, north London, and briefly in California, where he died tragically young at the age of 49.

John Lloyd was born in 1951 and first met Douglas at Cambridge University. They were friends for 30 years. John was the original producer of *The News Quiz*, *Quote . . . Unquote*, *To the Manor Born*, *Not the Nine O'Clock News*, *Blackadder*, *Spitting Image* and *QI*. He has also produced many books, including *The Book of General Ignorance*, which has been translated into 30 languages. He is married to Sarah and they have three children.

The Meaning of LIFF

42nd Anniversary Edition

DOUGLAS ADAMS

JOHN LLOYD

PAN BOOKS AND FABER AND FABER

This edition published with a new preface 2025 by Faber and Faber Limited and
Pan Books
an imprint of Pan Macmillan
The Smithson, 6 Briset Street, London EC1M 5NR
EU representative: Macmillan Publishers Ireland Ltd, 1st Floor,
The Liffey Trust Centre, 117–126 Sheriff Street Upper,
Dublin 1 D01 YC43
Associated companies throughout the world

ISBN 978-1-0350-5145-8

The Meaning of Liff first published 1983 by Pan Books and Faber and Faber;
and re-published with extra material as *The Deeper Meaning of Liff* 1990
by Pan Books and Faber and Faber.

With grateful thanks to Eugen Beer, Jane Belson, Jon Canter, Alex Catto,
Helen Fielding, Stephen Fry, Gaye Green, Sean Hardie, PBJ, Helen Rhys Jones,
Laurie Rowley, Peter Spence and Caroline Warner for some of the more
interesting and repellent ideas in this book.

1 3 5 7 9 8 6 4 2

A CIP catalogue record for this book is available from the British Library.

Map artwork by HL Studios

Printed and bound in the UK using 100% Renewable Electricity by CPI Group (UK)
Ltd

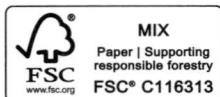

MIX
Paper | Supporting
responsible forestry
FSC® C116313
www.fsc.org

Visit **www.panmacmillan.com** to read more about
all our books and to buy them.

CONTENTS

Preface to the 42nd anniversary edition of *The Meaning of Liff*, 2025

In my early twenties, my best friend was a tall, clumsy genius called Douglas Adams (1952–2001).

In 1978, he had got stuck writing the first series for BBC Radio 4 of *The Hitchhiker's Guide to the Galaxy* and asked me to help him finish it.

We'd written together often before – so I said yes.

'I don't suppose there'll be a second series, Johnny,' he said, 'but, if there is, let's do it together.'

It had taken Douglas ten months to write the first four scripts, but we polished off the last two in three weeks.

The series was an instant success and before it had even finished going out we'd been invited to lunch by no less than six publishers.

We signed with Nick Webb at New English Library for £3,000 – half for each of us – and booked a month's holiday in Corfu to write it.

Then Douglas sacked me. He'd decided the

episodes we'd written together weren't as funny as the ones he'd written on his own.

I was blindsided, heartbroken and furious. I couldn't even look at him. 'Are you all right, Johnny?' he asked solicitously. And when I made it very clear I wasn't, he said, 'Why don't you get yourself an agent?'

So I went to see the redoubtable Marc Berlin, still my agent today and known (for his tough negotiating skills) as 'The Berlin Wall'.

He ran London Management, the largest entertainment agency in the country, and told me gleefully, 'We can take this guy for 10 per cent of anything with the name Hitchhiker on it for the rest of his life!' I was appalled.

'No, no,' I said, 'I just want my half of the advance for the book.' And we settled on that, though Douglas wasn't pleased.

'When I said, "Get yourself an agent," ' he yelled, 'I meant, "And write your own bloody book!" '

Astonishingly, given the acrimony between us, we set off for Greece together.

It was odd to begin with. Douglas would get up in the morning and sit at a table on the terrace in an enormous Terry Pratchett hat and start writing, while I went down to the windswept taverna on the beach from where the Great Novelist was visible to all.

By about 11am, the GN was creatively exhausted. He'd trudge down the hill and we'd tuck into a bottle of retsina and play games. Our favourite was one Douglas's old English master had introduced to his class in free periods, or at the end of term. 'What do you think Epping means?' he'd say. Or 'What do you think an Ely might be?'

Ely was the first definition we came up with – 'The first, tiniest inkling that something, somewhere, has gone terribly wrong.' It was so neat, so useful and so satisfying that we became hooked. I kept notes of all the best ones. Douglas failed to finish the book on that trip, and I went off to television to produce *Not the Nine O'Clock News*. In 1981, Robert McCrum, the editorial director of Faber and Faber, got in touch about publishing a spin-off joke-a-day calendar from the show. I took on the job of editor.

Though *Not the Nine* employed dozens of free-lance writers, finding two appropriate jokes for each day of the year (one for the front of each page and one for the back) was a huge task and I soon ran out of material. Scrabbling around for ideas, I found the notes of my chats with Douglas in 1978 and was surprised at how good the lines were.

Kettering *n*. The marks left on your bottom or

thighs after sitting sunbathing on a wickerwork chair. **Silloth** *n*. Something that was sticky and is now furry, found on the carpet under the sofa the morning after a party. **Motspur** *n*. The fourth wheel of a supermarket trolley which looks identical to the other three but renders the trolley completely uncontrollable.

I put these into the book – which was called *NOT 1982* – under the heading 'Today's new word from The Oxtail English Dictionary'.

When the proofs came out, Faber's chairman, Matthew Evans, said, 'There's one idea in here that stands out and could make a book in its own right – the dictionary definitions.'

I told friends about this and soon had a peremptory message from Douglas: 'Do nothing before you speak to me.'

So we wrote it jointly, co-published by Faber and Douglas's imprint Pan Books. By then, Douglas was an international smash, with *Hitchhiker* books selling by the million. In meetings with the publishers, my suggestions were met with polite indifference and Douglas's with rapturous admiration and applause.

I wanted the cover to scream, in bold letters: **'DOUGLAS ADAMS – THE HITCHHIKER'S GUIDE TO THE GLOSSARY.'**

I couldn't have cared less where, or how small,

my name appeared. Douglas, however, insisted on calling it *The Meaning of Liff*. This was because Monty Python had just released their film *The Meaning of Life* and he figured we might get extra sales from myopic people who thought it was the book of the movie.

To do him justice, he also insisted on equal billing (even though I argued no one would care, or even notice). Then there was the sizing. I was happy for it to be in a standard format, but Douglas was adamant it should be small enough to fit in a breast pocket. And completely black, like a prayer book.

That was what happened, even though creating a unique size cost the publishers money and annoyed booksellers because it was almost invisible to the naked eye.

Nonetheless, the first run sold an amazing third of a million copies – or, as Douglas despondently put it, 'only a third of a million'. It was well below the pay grade he'd become accustomed to.

The one advantage of the sizing was that we were able to adorn the back of later editions with three crisp reviews: 'Brilliant' – the *Times*; 'Brilliant' – the *Sunday Times*; and 'Small' – the *Cheshunt & Waltham Telegraph*.

Douglas died in 2001, impossibly young, at

only forty-nine. I have never borne him any ill will. Quite the reverse.

I have a saying I try to live by: Disaster is a Gift. If Douglas hadn't fired me from *Hitchhiker*, I'd probably never have done anything else and would have just been 'that bloke what's-his-name who works with Douglas Adams'.

Only the other day, a good friend of mine asked me if I'd ever read a book called *The Meaning of Liff*.

'Yes,' I said, 'I wrote it.' He looked astonished and pulled his dog-eared copy out of his pocket. He stared at the front cover in disbelief. 'Good Lord,' he said, 'I'd never noticed . . . '

John Lloyd, London, 2025

THE PREVIOUS PREFACES

Preface to the first edition, 1983
In Life* there are many hundreds of common
experiences, feelings, situations and even objects
which we all know and recognize, but for which no
word exists. On the other hand, the world is littered
with thousands of spare words which spend their
time doing nothing but loafing about on signposts
pointing at places. Our job, as we see it, is to get
these words down off the signposts and into the
mouths of babes and sucklings and so on, where
they can start earning their keep in everyday
conversation and make a more positive contribution
to society.
Douglas Adams, John Lloyd, Malibu, 1982

Preface to the 1984 reprint
What we said in the first preface pretty much stands,
I think.
Douglas Adams, New York, 1983

*And, indeed, in Liff.

Preface to the second 1984 reprint
Can't think of anything much to add to the previous
preface. It's nice, here, though.
Douglas Adams, Seychelles, 1984

Is it?
John Lloyd, Birmingham, 1984

Preface to the 1986 reprint
There was a point I was going to make in this
preface but it's one of those things that you just can't
remember when you actually sit down to write it.
Douglas Adams, Madagascar, 1985

Preface to the 1987 reprint
No. It came back to me briefly when I was in Brazil,
but I didn't have a pen with me.
Douglas Adams, Hong Kong, 1986

Preface to the 1988 reprint
Did you get the preface I faxed you from New
Zealand?
Douglas Adams, Zaïre, 1988

Preface to the 1989 reprint
No.
John Lloyd, Lambeth, 1989

Preface to the second 1989 reprint
Pity. That was a good one. Can't remember how it went now.
Douglas Adams, Beijing, 1989

Preface to the third 1989 reprint
Did we make the point about all these words actually being real place names?
Douglas Adams, Mauritius, 1989

Preface to the fourth 1989 reprint
Yes.
John Lloyd, Lambeth, 1989

Preface to the first edition of *The Deeper Meaning of Liff*, 1990
Well, there's not much we need to add to that then, really, is there?
Douglas Adams, John Lloyd, Sydney, 1990

Preface to the new edition of *The Meaning of Liff* incorporating *The Deeper Meaning of Liff*, 2013

Douglas, I've made a few small changes to acknowledge the passing of the years. Hope you're alive and well in some parallel universe – you're sadly missed in this one.
John Lloyd, Oxfordshire, 2013

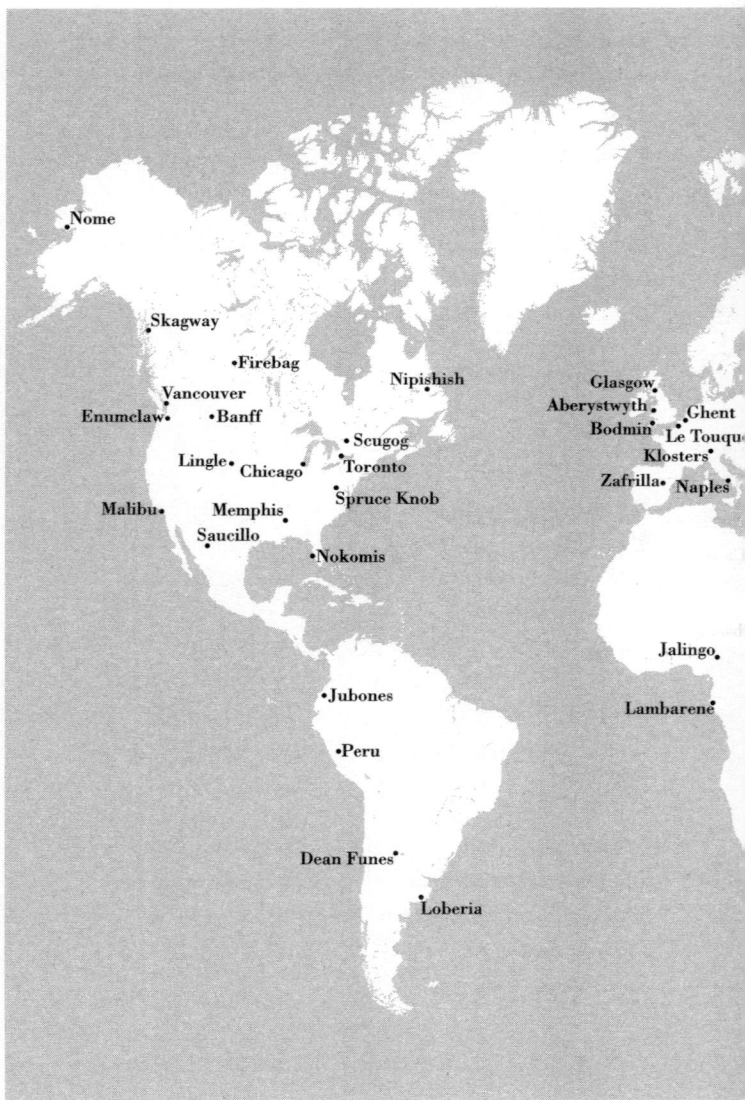

A

Aalst *n.*
One who changes his name to be nearer
the front.

Aasleagh *n.*
A liqueur made only for drinking at the end
of a revoltingly long bottle party when all the
drinkable drink has been drunk.

Abalemma *n.*
The agonizing situation in which there is only
one possible decision but you still can't take
it.

Aberbeeg *vb.*
Of amateur actors, to adopt a Mexican
accent when called upon to play any variety
of foreigner (except Pakistanis – for whom
a Welsh accent is considered sufficient).

Abercrave *vb.*
(ARCHAIC) To strongly desire to swing from
the pole at the back of a double-decker bus.

Abert *vb.*
To change a baby's name at the last possible
moment.

Aberystwyth *n.*
A nostalgic yearning which is in itself more
pleasant than the thing being yearned for.

Abilene *adj.*
Descriptive of the pleasing coolness on the
reverse side of the pillow.

Abinger *n.*
One who washes up everything except
the frying pan, the cheese-grater and the
saucepan which the chocolate sauce has been
made in.

Abligo *n.*
One who prides himself on not even knowing
what day of the week it is.

Aboyne *vb.*
To beat an expert at a game of skill by playing
so appallingly that none of his clever tactics
or strategies are of any use to him.

Abruzzo *n.*
The worn patch of ground under a swing.

Absecon *n.*
An annual conference held at the Dragonara
Hotel, Leeds, for people who haven't got any
other conferences to go to.

Abwong *vb.*
To bounce cheerfully on a bed.

Acklins *pl.n.*
The odd twinges you get in parts of your body
when you scratch other parts.

Acle *n.*
The rogue pin which shirtmakers conceal in
a hidden fold of a new shirt. Its function is to
stab you when you don the garment.

Addis Ababa *n.*
The torrent of incomprehensible gibberish
which emanates from the loudspeakers on top
of cars covered in stickers.

Adlestrop *n.*
The part of a suitcase which is designed to
get snarled up on conveyor belts at airports.
Some of the more modern adlestrop designs
have a special 'quick release' feature which
enables the case to flip open at this point
and fling your underclothes into the conveyor
belt's gearing mechanism.

Adrigole *n.*
The centre piece of a merry-go-round on
which the man with the tickets stands
unnervingly still.

Affcot *n.*
The sort of fart you hope people will talk after.

Affpuddle *n.*
A puddle which is hidden under a pivoted
paving stone. You only know it's there when
you step on the paving stone and the puddle
shoots up your leg.

Ahenny *adj.*
The way people stand when examining other people's bookshelves.

Aigburth *n.*
Any piece of readily identifiable anatomy found amongst cooked meat.

Ainderby Quernhow *n.*
One who continually bemoans the 'loss' of the word 'gay' to the English language, even though they had never used the word in any context at all until they started complaining that they couldn't use it any more.

Ainderby Steeple *n.*
One who asks you a question with the apparent motive of wanting to hear your answer, but who cuts short your opening sentence by leaning forward and saying, 'And I'll tell you why I ask . . .' and then talking solidly for the next hour.

Ainsworth *n.*
The length of time it takes to get served in
a mobile phone shop. Hence, also, how long
we'll have to wait for the Second Coming or
the abolition of income tax.

Aird of Sleat *n.*
(ARCHAIC) Ancient Scottish curse placed from
afar on the stretch of land now occupied by
Heathrow Airport.

Aith *n.*
The single bristle that sticks out sideways on
a cheap paintbrush.

Albacete *n.*
A single surprisingly long hair growing in the
middle of nowhere.

Albuquerque *n.*
The shapeless squiggle which is utterly
unlike your normal signature, but which is,
nevertheless, all you are able to produce
when asked formally to identify yourself.
Muslims, whose religion forbids the making of
graven images, use albuquerques to decorate
their towels, menu cards and pyjamas.

[6]

Alcoy *adj.*
Wanting to be bullied into having another
drink.

Aldclune *n.*
One who collects ten-year-old telephone
directories.

Alltami *n.*
The ancient art of being able to balance the
hot and cold shower taps.

Ambatolampy *n.*
The bizarre assortment of objects collected by
a sleepwalker.

Ambleside *n.*
The talk given about the Facts of Life by a
father to his son whilst walking in the garden
on a Sunday afternoon.

Amersham *n.*
The sneeze which tickles but never comes.
(Thought to derive from the Metropolitan Line
tube station of the same name where the rails
always rattle but the train never arrives.)

Amlwch *n.*
A British Rail sandwich which has been kept
soft by being regularly washed and resealed
in clingfilm.

Ampus *n.*
A lurid bruise which you can't remember
getting.

Anantnag *vb.*
(ESKIMO) To bang your thumbs between the
oars when rowing.

Anjozorobe *n.*
A loose, coloured garment someone brings
you back from their travels which they
honestly expect you to wear.

Araglin *n.*
(ARCHAIC) The medieval practical joke
played by young squires on a knight aspirant
the afternoon he is due to start his vigil. As
the knight arrives at the castle the squires
suddenly attempt to raise the drawbridge as
the knight and his charger step on it.

Ardcrony *n.*
A remote acquaintance passed off as 'a very good friend of mine' by someone trying to impress people.

Ardelve *vb.*
To make a big display of searching all your pockets when approached by a charity collector.

Ardentinny *n.*
One who rubs his hands eagerly together when he sits down in a restaurant.

Ardslignish *adj.*
Descriptive of the behaviour of Sellotape when you are tired.

Articlave *n.*
A clever architectural construction designed to give the illusion from the top deck of a bus that it is far too big for the road.

Ashdod *n.*
Any object against which a smoker habitually knocks out his pipe.

Aubusson *n.*
The hairstyle a girl adopts for a special
occasion which suddenly gives you a sense of
what she will look like in twenty years' time.

Aynho *vb.*
Of waiters, never to have a pen.

B

Babworth *n.*
Something which justifies having a really
good cry.

Badachonacher *n.*
An on–off relationship which never gets
resolved.

Badgebup *n.*
The splotch on a child's face where the
ice-cream cone has missed.

Baldock *n.*
The sharp prong on top of a tree stump
where the tree has snapped off before being
completely sawn through.

Balemartine *n.*
The look which says, 'Stop talking to that
woman at once.'

Ballycumber *n.*
One of the six half-read books lying somewhere in your bed.

Balzan *n.*
The noise of a dustbin lid coming off in the middle of the night.

Banff *adj.*
Pertaining to, or descriptive of, that kind of facial expression which is impossible to achieve except when having a passport photograph taken, which results in happas (q.v.).

Banteer *n.*
(ARCHAIC) A lusty and raucous old ballad sung after a particularly spectacular araglin (q.v.) has been pulled off.

Barstibley *n.*
(ARCHAIC) A device such as a china horse or small naked porcelain infant once used by jocular hosts to piss water into your Scotch.

Bathel *vb.*
To pretend to have read the book under discussion when in fact you've only seen the TV series.

Baughurst *n.*
That kind of large fierce ugly woman who owns a small fierce ugly dog.

Baumber *n.*
A fitted elasticated bottom sheet which turns your mattress banana-shaped.

Bauple *n.*
An indeterminate pustule which could be either a spot or a bite.

Bealings *pl.n.*
(ARCHAIC) The unsavoury parts of a moat which a knight has to pour out of his armour after being the victim of an araglin (q.v.). In medieval Flanders, soup made from bealings was a very slightly sought-after delicacy.

Beaulieu Hill *n.*
The optimum vantage point from which to
view people undressing in the bedroom across
the street.

Beccles *pl.n.*
The small bone buttons placed in bacon
sandwiches by unemployed dentists.

Bedfont *n.*
A lurching sensation in the pit of the stomach
experienced at breakfast in a hotel, occasioned
by the realization that it is about now that
the chambermaid will have discovered the
embarrassing stain on your bottom sheet.

Belding *n.*
The technical name for a stallion after its first
ball has been cut off. Any notice which reads
'Beware of the Belding' should be taken very,
very seriously.

Belper *n.*
A knob of someone else's chewing gum which
you unexpectedly find your hand resting on
under the passenger seat of your car or on
somebody's thigh under their skirt.

Benburb *n.*
The sort of man who becomes a returning officer.

Beppu *n.*
The triumphant slamming shut of a book after reading the final page.

Bepton *n.*
One who beams benignly after burping.

Berepper *n.*
The irrevocable and sturdy fart released in the presence of royalty, which sounds like quite a small motorbike passing by (but not enough to be confused with one).

Berkhamsted *n.*
The massive three-course midmorning blow-out enjoyed by a dieter who has already done his or her slimming duty by having a spoonful of cottage cheese for breakfast.

Berriwillock *n.*
An unknown workmate who writes 'All the best' on your leaving card.

Berry Pomeroy *n.*
1. The shape of a gourmet's lips.
2. The droplet of saliva which hangs from
them.

Bickerstaffe *n.*
The person in an office that everyone whinges
about in the pub. Corporate HR departments
actively recruit bickerstaffes and Lord Sugar
is both Chairman and Chief Bickerstaffe of
Amstrad plc.

Bilbster *n.*
A bauple (q.v.) so hideous and enormous that
you have to cover it with sticking plaster and
pretend you've cut yourself shaving.

Bindle *vb.*
To slip foreign coins into a customer's change.

Bishop's Caundle *n.*
An opening gambit before a game of chess
whereby the missing pieces are replaced by
small ornaments from the mantelpiece.

Blandford Forum *n.*
Any Radio 4 chat show.

Blean *n.*
Measure of luminosity: 1 glimmer = 100,000
bleans. The screen on a mobile phone
emits 150–500 bleans, enabling you to fall
downstairs or fracture your knee on the
furniture when using it as a torch.

Blithbury *n.*
A look someone gives you which indicates
that they're much too drunk to have
understood anything you've said to them
in the last twenty minutes.

Blitterlees *pl.n.*
The little slivers of bamboo picked off a
cane chair by a nervous guest which litter the
carpet beneath and tell the chair's owner that
the whole piece of furniture is about to uncoil
terribly and slowly until it resembles a giant
pencil sharpening.

Bodmin *n.*
The irrational and inevitable discrepancy
between the amount pooled and the amount
needed when a large group of people try to
pay a bill together after a meal.

Bogue *n.*
The expanse of skin that appears between
the top of your socks and the bottom of your
trousers when you sit down.

   'The Duke of Ilford threw himself onto
the chesterfield, brazenly displaying his
bogues to the dowager Lady Ingatestone.'
(*Come Soon, Strange Horseman*, by Barbara
Cartland.)

Boinka *n.*
The noise through the wall which tells you
that the people next door enjoy a better sex
life than you do.

Bolsover *n.*
One of those brown plastic trays with
bumps on, placed upside down in boxes of
chocolates to make you think you're getting
two layers.

Bonkle *vb.*
Of plumbing in old hotels, to make loud and
unexplained noises in the night, particularly
at about five o'clock in the morning.

Boolteens *pl.n.*
The small scattering of foreign coins and
1p pieces that inhabits dressing tables.

Boothby Graffoe *n.*
The man in the pub who slaps people on the
back as if they were old friends, when in fact
he has no friends, largely on account of this
habit.

Boscastle *n.*
(ARCHAIC) An enticing pyramid of
tinned tomatoes inside the entrance to a
supermarket.

Boseman *n.*
One who spends all day loafing about near
pedestrian crossings looking as if he's about
to cross.

Botcherby *n.*
The principle by which British roads are
signposted.

Botley *n.*
The prominent stain on a man's trouser crotch
seen on his return from the lavatory. A botley
proper is caused by an accident with the push
taps, and should not be confused with any
stain caused by insufficient waggling of the
willy (q.v. piddletrenthide).

Botolphs *pl.n.*
Huge benign tumours which archdeacons and
old chemistry teachers affect to wear on the
sides of their noses.

Botswana *n.*
Something which is more fruitfully used for
a purpose other than that for which it was
designed. A fishknife used to lever open a
stubborn tin of emulsion is a fine example
of a botswana.

Botusfleming *n.*
(MEDICAL) A small, long-handled steel trowel
used by surgeons to remove the contents of a
patient's nostrils prior to a sinus operation.

Brabant *adj.*
Very much inclined to see how far you can push someone.

Bradford *n.*
A schoolteacher's old hairy jacket, now severely discoloured by chalk dust, ink, egg and the precipitations of unedifying chemical reactions.

Bradworthy *n.*
One who is skilled in the art of naming loaves.

Breckles *n.*
A disease of artificial plants.

Brecon *n.*
The part of the toenail which is designed to snag on nylon sheets.

Brindle *vb.*
To remember suddenly where it is you're meant to be going after you've already been driving for ten minutes.

Brisbane *n.*
A perfectly reasonable explanation. (Such as one offered by a person with a gurgling cough which has nothing to do with the fact that they smoke fifty cigarettes a day.)

Brithdir *n.*
(OLD NORSE) The first day of the winter on which your breath condenses in the air.

Broats *pl.n.*
Trousers with a history: broats are most often seen on elderly retired army officers. Originally part of their best suit in the 50s; in the 70s they were demoted and used for gardening. Recently, pensions not being what they were, the broats have been called out of retirement and reinstated as part of the best suit again.

Brompton *n.*
A brompton is that which is said to have been committed when you are convinced you are about to blow off with a resounding trumpeting noise in a public place and all that actually slips out is a tiny 'pfpt'.

Bromsgrove *n.*
Any urban environment containing a small amount of dog turd and about forty-five tons of bent steel pylon or a lump of concrete with holes claiming to be sculpture.

'Oh, come my dear, and come with me
And wander 'neath the bromsgrove tree' –
Betjeman

Brough Sowerby *n.*
One who has been working at the same desk in the same office for fifteen years and has very much his own ideas about why he is continually passed over for promotion.

Brumby *n.*
The fake antique plastic seal on a pretentious whisky bottle.

Brymbo *n.*
The single unappetizing bun left in a baker's shop after four p.m.

Budby *n.*
A nipple clearly defined through flimsy or wet material.

Bude *n.*
A polite joke reserved for use in the presence of vicars.

Budle *vb.*
To fart underwater.

Buldoo *n.*
A virulent red-coloured pus which generally accompanies clonmult (q.v.) and sadberge (q.v.).

Burbage *n.*
The sound made by a liftful of people all trying to breathe through their noses.

Bures *pl.n.*
(MEDICAL) The scabs on the knees and elbows formed by a compulsion to make love on cheap floor-matting.

Burleston *n.*
That peculiarly tuneless humming and whistling adopted by people who are extremely angry.

Burlingjobb *n.*
(ARCHAIC) A seventeenth-century crime by
which excrement is thrown into the street
from a ground-floor window.

Burnt Yates *pl.n.*
Condition to which yates (q.v.) will suddenly
pass without any apparent intervening period,
after the spirit of the throckmorton (q.v.)
has finally been summoned by incessant
throcking (q.v.).

Bursledon *n.*
The bluebottle one is too tired to get up and
swat, but not tired enough to sleep through.

Burslem *n.*
One who goes on talking at three o'clock in
the morning after everyone else has gone to
sleep. The principal habitat of burslems is
Radio 2.

Burton Coggles *pl.n.*
The bunch of keys found in a drawer whose
purpose has long been forgotten, and which
can therefore now be used only for dropping
down people's backs as a cure for nose-bleeds.

Burwash *n.*
The pleasurable cool sloosh of puddle water
over the toes of your gumboots.

C

Caarnduncan *n.*
The high-pitched and insistent cry of the
young male human urging one of its peer
group to do something dangerous on a cliff-
edge or piece of toxic waste ground.

Cadomin *n.*
The ingredient in coffee creamer that rises
to the surface as scum.

Cafu *n.*
The frustration of not being able to remember
what an acronym stands for.

Cahors *pl.n.*
The rushes of emotion triggered by overheard
snatches of an old song.

Cairo *n.*
The noise of a spinning hub cap coming
to rest.

Calicut *adj.*
Determined not to let someone see how much their inadvertent remark has hurt you.

Camer *n.*
A mis-tossed caber.

Cannock Chase *n.*
In any box of After Eight Mints, there is always a large number of empty envelopes and no more than four or five actual mints. The cannock chase is the process by which, no matter which part of the box you insert your fingers into, or how often, you will always extract most of the empty sachets before pinning down an actual mint, or 'cannock'.

The cannock chase also occurs with people who put dead matches back in the matchbox, and then embarrass themselves at parties trying to light cigarettes with three quarters of an inch of charcoal.

The term is also used to describe futile attempts to pursue unscrupulous advertising agencies who nick your ideas to sell chocolates with.

Canudos *n.*
The desire of married couples to see their single friends pair off.

Chaling *ptcpl.vb.*
Trying not to be driven up the wall by the opinions of someone whom circumstances will not allow you to argue with.

Cheb *n.*
An embarrassing nickname by which a fourteen-year-old boy insists that he now wishes to be known.

Chenies *pl.n.*
The last few sprigs or tassels of last year's Christmas decorations you notice on the ceiling while lying on the sofa on an August afternoon.

Chicago *n.*
The foul-smelling wind which precedes an underground train.

Chimbote *n.*
A newly fashionable ethnic stew which,
however much everyone raves about it, seems
to you to have rather a lot of fish-heads in it.

Chimkent *n.*
One whose life appears not to have moved on
in any direction at all when you meet them
again ten years later.

Chipping Ongar *n.*
The disgust and embarrassment (or 'ongar')
felt by an observer in the presence of a
person festooned with kirbies (q.v.), when
they don't know them well enough to tell
them to wipe them off. Invariably this 'ongar'
is accompanied by an involuntary staccato
twitching of the leg (or 'chipping').

Clabby *n.*
A desultory, stilted and mutually
condescending conversation between a
middle-class person and their cleaner.

Clackavoid *n.*
The technical term for a single page of script
from an Australian soap opera.

Clackmannan *n.*
The sound made by knocking over an
elephant's-foot umbrella-stand full of
walking-sticks.

Clathy *adj.*
Nervously indecisive about how to dispose
of a dud lightbulb.

Clenchwarton *n.*
(ARCHAIC) One who assists an exorcist by
squeezing whichever part of the possessed
the exorcist deems useful.

Climpy *adj.*
Allowing yourself to be persuaded to do
something and pretending to be reluctant.

Clingman's Dome *n.*
The condition in which it becomes impossible
to put on a tie correctly when in a hurry for an
important meeting.

Clixby *adj.*
Politely rude. Briskly vague. Firmly
uninformative.

Cloates Point *n.*
The precise instant at which scrambled eggs are ready.

Clonmult *n.*
A yellow ooze usually found near secretions of buldoo (q.v.) and sadberge (q.v.).

Clovis *n.*
One who actually looks forward to putting up the Christmas decorations in the office.

Clun *n.*
A leg which has gone to sleep and has to be hauled around after you.

Clunes *pl.n.*
People who just won't go.

Coilantogle *n.*
(VULGAR) Long elasticated loop of snot which connects a pulled bogey to a nose.

Condover *n.*
One who is employed to stand about all day browsing through the magazine rack in the newsagent.

Cong *n.*
Strange-shaped metal utensil found at
the back of the saucepan cupboard. Many
authorities believe that congs provide
conclusive proof of the existence of a now
extinct form of yellow vegetable which the
Victorians used to boil mercilessly.

Coodardy *adj.*
Astounded at what you've just managed to
get away with.

Corfe *n.*
An object which is almost totally
indistinguishable from a newspaper, the
one crucial difference being that it belongs
to somebody else and is unaccountably
more interesting than your own – which
may otherwise appear to be in all respects
identical.
　　Though it is a rule of life that a train or
other public place may contain any number
of corfes but only one newspaper, it is quite
possible to transform your own perfectly
ordinary newspaper into a corfe by the simple
expedient of letting someone else read it.

Corfu *n.*
The dullest person you met during the course of your holiday. Also the only one who failed to understand that the exchanging of addresses at the end of the holiday is merely a social ritual and is absolutely not an invitation to phone you up or turn up unannounced on your doorstep three months later.

Corriearklet *n.*
The moment at which two people, approaching from opposite ends of a long passageway, recognize each other and immediately pretend they haven't. This is to avoid the ghastly embarrassment of having to continue recognizing each other the whole length of the corridor.

Corriecravie *n.*
To avert the horrors of corrievorrie (q.v.), corriecravie is usually employed. This is the cowardly but highly skilled process by which both protagonists continue to approach while keeping up the pretence that they haven't noticed each other – by staring furiously at their feet, grimacing into a notebook, or studying the walls closely as if in a mood of deep irritation.

Corriedoo *n.*
The crucial moment of false recognition in
a long passageway encounter. Though both
people are perfectly well aware that the other
is approaching, they must eventually pretend
sudden recognition. They now look up with
a glassy smile, as if having spotted each
other for the first time (and are particularly
delighted to have done so), shouting out,
'Haaaaalllllloooo!' as if to say, 'Good grief!!
You!! Here!! Of all people! Well I never. Coo.
Stap me vitals,' etcetera.

Corriemoillie *n.*
The dreadful sinking sensation in a long
passageway encounter when both protagonists
immediately realize they have plumped for
the corriedoo (q.v.) much too early as they
are still a good thirty yards apart. They were
embarrassed by the pretence of corriecravie
(q.v.) and decided to make use of the
corriedoo because they felt silly. This was a
mistake as corrievorrie (q.v.) will make them
seem far sillier.

Corriemuchloch *n.*
The kind of person who can make a complete mess of a simple job like walking down a corridor.

Corrievorrie *n.*
Corridor etiquette demands that once a corriedoo (q.v.) has been declared, corrievorrie must be employed. Both protagonists must now embellish their approach with an embarrassing combination of waving, grinning, making idiot faces, doing pirate impressions, and waggling the head from side to side while holding the other person's eyes as the smile drips off their face, until, with great relief, they pass each other.

Corstorphine *n.*
A very short peremptory service held in monasteries prior to tea-time to offer thanks for the benediction of digestive biscuits.

Cotterstock *n.*
A piece of wood used to stir paint and thereafter stored uselessly in the shed in perpetuity.

Cowcaddens *pl.n.*
A set of twelve cowcaddens makes an ideal
and completely baffling wedding gift.

Craboon *vb.*
To shout boisterously from a cliff.

Crail *n.*
Crail is a common kind of rock or gravel
found widely across the British Isles.
    Each individual stone (due to an as yet
undiscovered gravitational property) is
charged with 'negative buoyancy'. This means
that no matter how much crail you remove
from the garden, more of it will rise to the
surface.
    Crail is much employed by the Royal Navy
for making the paperweights and ashtrays
used in submarines.

Cranleigh *n.*
A mood of irrational irritation with everyone
and everything.

Cresbard *n.*
The light working lunch which Anne
Hathaway used to make for her husband.

Crieff *vb.*
To agree sycophantically with a taxi-driver about immigration.

Cromarty *n.*
The brittle sludge which clings to the top of ketchup bottles and plastic tomatoes in nasty cafés.

D

Dalderby *n.*
A letter to the editor made meaningless
because it refers to a previous letter you
didn't read. (See A.H. Hedgehope, July 3rd.)

Dalfibble *vb.*
To spend large swathes of your life looking for
car keys.

Dallow *adj.*
Perfectly content to stare at something for no
particular reason.

Dalmilling *ptcpl.vb.*
Continually making small talk to someone
who is trying to read a book.

Dalrymple *n.*
Dalrymples are the things you pay extra for on pieces of handmade craftwork – the rough edges, the paint smudges and the holes in the glazing.

Damnaglaur *n.*
A certain facial expression which actors are required to demonstrate their mastery of before they are allowed to play Macbeth.

Darenth *n.*
Measure = 0.0000176 mg.
   Defined as that amount of margarine capable of covering one hundred slices of bread to the depth of one molecule. This is the legal maximum allowed in sandwich bars in Greater London.

Darvel *vb.*
To hold out hope for a better invitation until the last possible moment.

Dattuck *n.*
One who performs drum solos on his knees.

Deal *n.*
The gummy substance found between
damp toes.

Dean Funes *pl.n.*
Things that clergymen opine on that are
none of their damn business.

Delaware *n.*
The hideous stuff on the shelves of a rented
house.

Des Moines *pl.n.*
The two little lines that come down from
your nose.

Detchant *n.*
The part of the hymn (usually a few notes at
the end of the verse) where the tune goes so
high or low that you suddenly have to change
pitch to accommodate it.

Deventer *n.*
A decision that's very hard to take because so
little depends on it – like which way to walk
round a park.

Dewlish *adj.*
(Of the hands and feet.) Prunelike after an
overlong bath.

Didcot *n.*
The tiny oddly shaped bit of card which
a ticket inspector cuts out of a ticket with
his clipper for no apparent reason. It is
a little-known fact that the confetti at
Princess Margaret's wedding was made up of
thousands of didcots collected by inspectors
on the Royal Train.

Dillytop *n.*
The kind of bath plug which for some
unaccountable reason is actually designed to
sit on top of the hole rather than fit into it.

Dinder *vb.*
To nod thoughtfully while someone gives you
a long and complex set of directions which
you know you're never going to remember.

Dinsdale *n.*
One who always plays 'Chopsticks' on
the piano.

Dipple *vb.*
To try to remove a sticky something from
one hand with the other, thus causing it to
get stuck to the other hand and eventually
to anything else you try to remove it with.

Ditherington *n.*
Sudden access of panic experienced by
one who realizes that he is being drawn
inexorably into a clabby (q.v.) conversation,
i.e. one he has no hope of enjoying, benefiting
from or understanding.

Dobwalls *pl.n.*
The now hard-boiled bits of nastiness which
have to be prised off crockery by hand after
it has been through a dishwasher.

Dockery *n.*
Facetious behaviour adopted by an accused
man in the mistaken belief that this will
endear him to the judge.

Dogdyke *vb.*
Of dog owners, to adopt the absurd pretence
that the animal shitting in the gutter is
nothing to do with them.

Dolgellau *n.*
The clump, or cluster, of bored, quietly enraged, mildly embarrassed men waiting for their wives to come out of a changing room in a dress shop.

Dorchester *n.*
Someone else's throaty cough which obscures the crucial part of the rather amusing remark you've just made.

Dorridge *n.*
Technical term for one of the very lame excuses written in very small print on the side of packets of food or washing powder to explain why there's hardly anything inside. Examples include 'Contents may have settled in transit' and 'To keep biscuits fresh they have been individually wrapped in silver paper and cellophane and separated with corrugated lining, a cardboard flap, and heavy industrial tyres.'

Draffan *n.*
An infuriating person who always manages to look much more dashing than anyone else by turning up unshaven and hungover at a formal party.

Drebley *n.*
Name for a shop which is supposed to be witty but is in fact wearisome, e.g. 'The Frock Exchange', 'Hair Apparent', etc.

Droitwich *n.*
A street dance. The two partners approach from opposite directions and try politely to get out of each other's way. They step to the left, step to the right, apologize, step to the left again, bump into each other and repeat as often as unnecessary.

Drumsna *n.*
The earthquake that occurs when a character in a cartoon runs into a wall.

Dubbo *n.*
The bruise or callus on the shoulder of someone who has been knighted unnecessarily often.

Dubuque *n.*
A look given by a superior person to someone who has arrived wearing the wrong sort of shoes.

Duddo *n.*
The most deformed potato in any given
collection of potatoes.

Dufton *n.*
The last page of a document that you always
leave face down in the photocopier and have
to go and retrieve later.

Duggleby *n.*
The person in front of you in the supermarket
queue who has just unloaded a bulging trolley
on to the conveyor belt and is now in the
process of trying to work out which pocket
they left their cheque book in, and indeed,
which pair of trousers.

Duleek *n.*
Sudden realization, as you lie in bed waiting
for the alarm to go off, that it should have
gone off an hour ago.

Duluth *adj.*
The smell of a taxi out of which people have
just got.

Dunbar *n.*
A highly specialized fiscal term used solely
by turnstile operatives at London Zoo.

Dunboyne *n.*
The realization that the train you have
patiently watched pulling out of the station
was the one you were meant to be on.

Duncraggon *n.*
Chuck Norris's retirement cottage.

Dungeness *n.*
The uneasy feeling that the plastic handles
of the overloaded supermarket carrier-bag
you are carrying are getting steadily longer.

Dunino *n.*
Someone who always wants to do whatever
you want to do.

Dunolly *n.*
An improvised umbrella.

Dunster *n.*
A small child hired to bounce at dawn on the occupants of the spare bedroom in order to save on tea and alarm clocks.

Duntish *adj.*
Mentally incapacitated by a severe hangover.

E

Eads *pl.n.*
The sludgy bits in the bottom of a dustbin, underneath the actual bin liner.

Eakring *ptcpl.vb.*
Wondering what to do next when you've just stormed out of something.

East Wittering *n.*
The same as West Wittering (q.v.), only it's you they're trying to get away from.

Edgbaston *n.*
(ARCHAIC) Seat-cushion from a bus removed by the driver and leant against the rear of the vehicle to indicate it has broken down.

Elgin *adj.*
Thin and haggard as a result of strenuously trying to get healthy.

Elsrickle *n.*
A bead of sweat which runs down your bottom cleavage.

Ely *n.*
The first, tiniest inkling that something, somewhere, has gone terribly wrong.

Emsworth *n.*
Measure of time and noiselessness defined as the moment between the doors of a lift closing and it beginning to move. Scientists believe we spend up to one fifth of our lives in lifts.

Enumclaw *n.*
One of the initiation rituals of the Freemasons which they are no longer allowed to do.

Epping *ptcpl.vb.*
The futile movements of forefingers and eyebrows used when failing to attract the attention of waiters and barmen.

Epsom *n.*
An entry in a diary (such as a date or a set of initials) or a name and address in your address book, of which you haven't the faintest idea what it's doing there.

Epworth *n.*
The precise value of the usefulness of epping (q.v.). It is a little-known fact that an earlier draft of the final line of the film *Gone with the Wind* had Clark Gable saying, 'Frankly, my dear, I don't give an epworth,' the line being eventually changed on the grounds that it might not be understood in Iowa, or indeed anywhere.

Eriboll *n.*
A brown bubble of cheese containing gaseous matter which grows on welsh rarebit. It was Sir Alexander Fleming's study of eribolls which led, indirectly, to his discovery of the fact that he didn't like welsh rarebit much.

Esher *n.*
A rogue push tap in a public washroom.
The most powerful esher of recent years
was 'damped down' by a team of Texan
roustabouts after an incredible 68-day fight
in Manchester's Piccadilly Station.

Essendine *n.*
Long slow sigh emitted by a fake leather
armchair when sat on.

Esterhazy *adj.*
(MEDICAL) Suffering from selective memory
loss. The virus which causes this condition
is thought to breed in the air-conditioning
system of the White House.

Euphrates *n.*
The bullshit with which a chairman
introduces a guest speaker.

Evercreech *n.*
The collective glare of a group of polite, angry
people at a rude, calm queue-barger.

Ewelme *n.*
The smile bestowed on you by an air hostess.

Exeter *n.*

All light household and electrical goods
contain a number of vital components plus at
least one exeter.

If you've just mended a fuse, changed a
bulb or fixed a blender, the exeter is the small
plastic piece left over which means you have
to undo everything and start all over again.

F

Falster *n.*
A long-winded, dishonest and completely
incredible excuse used when the truth would
have been completely acceptable.

Famagusta *n.*
The draught which whistles between two
bottoms that refuse to touch.

Farduckmanton *n.*
(ARCHAIC) An ancient edict, mysteriously
omitted from the Domesday Book, requiring
that the feeding of fowl on village ponds
should be carried out equitably.

Farnham *n.*
The feeling that you get at about four o'clock
in the afternoon when you haven't got enough
done.

Farrancassidy *n.*
A long and ultimately unsuccessful attempt
to undo someone's bra.

Fentonadle *vb.*
To lay place settings with the knives and
forks the wrong way round.

Ferfer *n.*
One who is very excited that they've had
a better idea than the one you've just
suggested.

Finuge *vb.*
In any division of foodstuffs equally between
several people, to give yourself the extra slice
left over.

Firebag *n.*
A remark intended to cue applause at a Tory
party conference.

Fiunary *n.*
The safe place you put something and forget
where it was.

Fladderbister *n.*
That part of a raincoat which trails out of
a car after you've closed the door on it.

Flagler *n.*
Someone who always seems to disappear
into shops when you're walking along talking
to them.

Flimby *n.*
One of those irritating handle-less slippery
translucent bags you get in supermarkets
which, no matter how you hold them, always
contrive to let something fall out.

Flodigarry *n.*
(SCOTS) An ankle-length oilskin worn
by deep-sea fishermen in Arbroath and
publicans in Glasgow.

Flums *pl.n.*
Women who only talk to each other at parties.

Foffarty *adj.*
Unable to find the right moment to leave.

Foindle *vb.*
To queue-jump very discreetly by working one's way up the line without being spotted doing so.

Foping *ptcpl.vb.*
Refusing to say what it is you're looking so bloody wistful about.

Forsinain *n.*
(ARCHAIC) The right of the lord of the manor to molest dwarfs on their birthdays.

Fovant *n.*
A taxi-driver's gesture, a raised hand pointed out of the window which purports to mean 'thank you' but actually means 'bugger off out of my way'.

Fraddam *n.*
The small awkward-shaped piece of cheese which remains after grating a large regular-shaped piece of cheese, and which enables you to grate your fingers.

Framlingham *n.*
A kind of burglar alarm in common usage.
It is cunningly designed so that it can ring at
full volume in the street without apparently
disturbing anyone.

Other types of framlinghams are burglar
alarms fitted to business premises in
residential areas, which go off as a matter
of regular routine at 5.31 p.m. on a Friday
evening and do not get turned off till
9.20 a.m. on Monday morning.

Frant *n.*
Measure. The legal minimum distance
between two trains on the District and Circle
lines of the London Underground. A frant,
which must be not less than 122 chains (or
8 leagues) long, is not connected in any way
with the adjective 'frantic' which comes to us
by a completely different route (as indeed do
the trains).

Frating Green *adj.*
The shade of green which is supposed to
make you feel comfortable in hospitals,
industrious in schools and uneasy in police
stations.

Frimley *n.*
Exaggerated carefree saunter adopted by
Norman Wisdom as an immediate prelude to
dropping down an open manhole.

Fring *n.*
The noise made by a lightbulb that has just
shone its last.

Fritham *n.*
A paragraph that you get stuck on in a book.
The more you read it, the less it means to you.

Frolesworth *n.*
Measure. The minimum time it is necessary
to spend frowning in deep concentration at
each picture in an art gallery in order that
everyone else doesn't think you're a complete
moron.

Frosses *pl.n.*
The lecherous looks exchanged between
sixteen-year-olds at a party given by
someone's parents.

Frutal *adj.*
Rather too eager to be cruel to be kind.

Fulking *ptcpl.vb.*
Pretending not to be in when the carol-singers come round.

G

Gaffney *n.*
Someone who deliberately misunderstands
things for, he hopes, humorous effect.

Galashiels *pl.n*
A form of particularly long sparse sideburns
which are part of the mandatory turnout of
steam-train drivers.

Gallipoli *adj.*
Of the behaviour of a bottom lip trying to
spit out mouthwash after an injection at
the dentist. Hence, loose, floppy, useless.

'She went all gallipoli in his arms' – Noel
Coward

Gammersgill *n.*
Embarrassed stammer you emit when a voice
answers the phone and you realize that you
haven't the faintest recollection of who it is
you've just rung.

Garrow *n.*
Narrow wiggly furrow left after pulling a hair off a painted surface.

Gartness *n.*
The ability to say, 'No, there's absolutely nothing the matter, what could possibly be the matter? And anyway I don't want to discuss it,' without moving your lips.

Garvock *n.*
The action of putting your finger in your cheek and flicking it out with a 'pock' noise.

Gastard *n.*
Useful specially new-coined word for an illegitimate child (in order to distinguish it from someone who merely carves you up on the motorway, etc.).

Ghent *adj.*
Descriptive of the mood indicated by cartoonists by drawing a character's mouth as a wavy line.

Gignog *n.*
Someone who, through the injudicious
application of alcohol, is now a great deal
less funny than he thinks he is.

Gildersome *adj.*
Descriptive of a joke someone tells you
which starts well, but which becomes so
embellished in the telling that you start to
weary of it after scarcely half an hour.

Gilgit *n.*
Hidden sharply pointed object which stabs
you in the cuticle when you reach into a
small pot.

Gilling *n.*
The warm tingling you get in your feet when
having a really good widdle.

Gipping *ptcpl.vb.*
The fish-like opening and closing of the
jaws seen amongst people who have recently
been to the dentist and are puzzled as to
whether their teeth have been put back the
right way up.

Glasgow *n.*
The feeling of infinite sadness engendered
when walking through a place filled with
happy people fifteen years younger than
yourself. When experienced too frequently, it
is likely to lead to an attack of trunch (q.v.).

Glassel *n.*
A seaside pebble which was shiny and
interesting when wet, and which is now a
lump of rock, which children nevertheless
insist on filling their suitcases with after
the holiday.

Glazeley *adj.*
The state of a barrister's flat greasy hair after
wearing a wig all day.

Glemanuilt *n.*
The kind of guilt which you'd completely
forgotten about which comes roaring back
on discovering an old letter in a cupboard.

Glenduckie *n.*
Any Scottish actor who wears a cravat.

Glentaggart *n.*
A particular type of tartan hold-all, made
exclusively under licence for British Airways.
　　When waiting to collect your luggage
from an airport conveyor belt, you will notice
that on the next conveyor belt along there
is always a single, solitary bag going round
and round uncollected. This is a glentaggart,
which has been placed there by the baggage-
handling staff to take your mind off the fact
that your own luggage will shortly be landing
in Murmansk.

Glenties *pl.n.*
Series of small steps by which someone
who has made a serious tactical error in
conversation or argument moves from
complete disagreement to wholehearted
agreement.

Glenwhilly *n.*
(SCOTS) A small tartan pouch worn beneath
the kilt during the thistle-harvest.

Glinsk *n.*
A hat which politicians buy to go to Russia in.

Glororum *n.*
One who takes pleasure in informing others
about their bowel movements.

Glossop *n.*
A rogue blob of food. Glossops, which are
generally steaming hot and highly adhesive,
invariably fall off your spoon and on to the
surface of your host's highly polished antique
rosewood dining table. If this has not, or
may not have, been noticed by the company
present, swanage (q.v.) may be employed.

Glud *n.*
The pinkish mulch found in the bottom of a
lady's handbag.

Glutt Lodge *n.*
The place where food can be stored after
having a tooth extracted. Nomadic tribesmen
can go without sustenance for up to six weeks
on a full glutt lodge.

Godalming *n.*
Wonderful rush of relief on discovering that
the ely (q.v.) and the wembley (q.v.) were in
fact false alarms.

Goginan *n.*
The piece of Elastoplast on a short-sighted child's spectacles.

Golant *adj.*
Blank, sly and faintly embarrassed.
Pertaining to the expression seen on the face of someone who has clearly forgotten your name.

Gonnabarn *n.*
An afternoon wasted on watching an old movie on TV.

Goole *n.*
The puddle on the bar into which the barman puts your change.

Goosecruives *pl.n.*
(ARCHAIC) A pair of wooden trousers worn by poultry-keepers in the Middle Ages.

Goosnargh *n.*
Something left over from preparing or eating a meal, which you store in the fridge despite the fact that you know full well that you will never ever use it.

Great Tosson *n.*
A fat book containing four words and six cartoons priced at £14.99.

Great Wakering *ptcpl.vb.*
Panic which sets in when you badly need to go to the lavatory and cannot make up your mind about what book or magazine to take with you.

Greeley *n.*
Someone who continually annoys you by continually apologizing for annoying you.

Gress *vb.*
(RARE) To stick to the point during a family argument.

Gretna Green *adj.*
A shade of green which makes you wish you'd painted whatever it was a different colour.

Gribun *n.*
The person in a crisis who can always be relied on to make a good anecdote out of it.

Grimbister *n.*
Large body of cars on a motorway all
travelling at exactly the speed limit because
one of them is a police car.

Grimmet *n.*
A small bush from which cartoon characters
dangle over the edge of a cliff.

Grimsby *n.*
A lump of something gristly and foul-tasting
concealed in a mouthful of stew or pie.

    Grimsbies are sometimes merely the result
of careless cookery, but more often they are
placed there deliberately by Freemasons.
Grimsbies can be purchased in bulk from
any respectable Masonic butcher on giving
him the secret Masonic handbag. One is then
placed in a guest's food to see if he knows the
correct Masonic method of dealing with it.

    This is as follows: remove the grimsby
carefully with the silver tongs provided.
Cross the room to your host, hopping on one
leg, and ram the grimsby firmly up his nose,
chanting, 'Take that, you smug Masonic
bastard.'

Grinstead *n.*
The state of a woman's clothing after she has
been to powder her nose and has hitched
up her tights over her skirt at the back, thus
exposing her bottom, and has walked out
without noticing it.

Grobister *n.*
One who continually and publicly rearranges
the position of his genitals.

Gruids *n.*
The only bits of an animal left after even the
people who make sausage rolls have been at
it.

Grutness *n.*
The resolve with which the Queen sits
through five days of Polynesian folk dancing.

Gubblecote *n.*
Deformation of the palate caused by biting
into too many Toblerones.

Guernsey *adj.*
Queasy but unbowed. The kind of feeling one
gets when discovering a plastic compartment
in a fridge in which things are growing,
usually fertilized by copious quantities of
goosnargh (q.v.).

Gulberwick *n.*
The small particle that you always think
you've got stuck in the back of your throat
after you've been sick.

Gussage *n.*
Dress-making talk.

Gweek *n.*
A coat hanger recycled as a car aerial.

H

Hadweenzic *adj.*
Resistant to tweezers.

Hadzor *n.*
A sharp instrument placed in the washing-up
bowl which makes it easier to cut yourself.

Hagnaby *n.*
Someone who looked a lot more attractive in
the disco than they do in your bed the next
morning.

Halcro *n.*
An adhesive cloth designed to fasten baby-
clothes together. Thousands of tiny pieces
of jam 'hook' on to thousands of pieces of
dribble, enabling the cloth to become 'sticky'.

Halifax *n.*
The green synthetic AstroTurf on which
greengrocers display their vegetables.

Hallspill *n.*
The name for the adventurous partygoers who
don't spend the whole time in the kitchen.

Hambledon *n.*
The sound of a single-engined aircraft flying
by, heard while lying in a summer field in
England, which somehow concentrates the
silence and sense of space and timelessness
and leaves one with the feeling of something
or other.

Hankate *adj.*
Congenitally incapable of ever having a paper
tissue.

Happas *n.*
The amusement caused by passport photos.

Happle *vb.*
To annoy people by finishing their sentences
for them and then telling them what they
really meant to say.

Harbledown *vb.*
To manoeuvre a double mattress down a
winding staircase.

Harbottle *n.*
A particular kind of fly which lives inside double glazing.

Harlosh *vb.*
To redistribute the hot water in a bath.

Harmanger *n.*
The person who takes the blame while the manager you demanded to see hides in his office.

Harpenden *n.*
The coda to a phone conversation, consisting of about eight exchanges, by which people try gracefully to get off the line.

Haselbury Plucknett *n.*
A mechanical device for cleaning combs invented during the industrial revolution at the same time as Arkwright's Spinning Jenny, but which didn't catch on in the same way.

Hassop *n.*
The pocket down the back of an armchair used for storing 10p pieces and bits of Lego.

Hastings *pl.n.*
Things said on the spur of the moment to
explain to someone who unexpectedly comes
into a room precisely what it is you are doing.

Hathersage *n.*
The tiny snippets of beard which coat the
inside of a wash-basin after shaving in it.

Haugham *n.*
One who loudly informs other diners in a
restaurant what kind of man he is by calling
the chef by his Christian name from the lobby.

Haxby *n.*
Any gardening implement found in a potting-
shed whose exact purpose is unclear.

Heanton Punchardon *n.*
A violent argument which breaks out in the
car on the way home from a party between
a couple who have had to be polite to each
other in company all evening.

Henstridge *n.*
A dried yellow substance found between the
prongs of forks in restaurants.

Hepple *vb.*
To sculpt the contents of a sugar bowl.

Herstmonceux *n.*
The correct name for the gold medallion worn by someone who is in the habit of wearing their shirt open to the waist.

Hessle *vb.*
To try and sort out which sleeve of a sweater is inside out when you're already half-way through putting it on.

Hever *n.*
The panic caused by half-hearing a Tannoy in an airport.

Hewish *adj.*
In a mood to swipe at vegetation with a stick.

Hextable *n.*
The record you find in someone else's collection which instantly tells you you could never go out with them.

Hibbing *n.*
The marks left on the outside breast pocket of a storekeeper's overall where he put away his pen and missed.

Hickling *ptcpl.vb.*
The practice of infuriating theatre-goers by not only arriving late to a centre-row seat, but also loudly apologizing to and patting each member of the audience in turn.

Hidcote Bartram *n.*
To be caught in a hidcote bartram is to say a series of protracted and final goodbyes to a group of people and then realize that you've left your hat behind.

High Limerigg *n.*
The topmost tread of a staircase which disappears when you're climbing the stairs in darkness.

High Offley *n.*
Goosnargh (q.v.) three weeks later.

Hobarris *n.*
(MEDICAL) A sperm which carries a high risk of becoming a bank manager.

Hobbs Cross *n.*
The awkward leaping manoeuvre a girl has to go through in bed in order to make him sleep on the wet patch.

Hoddlesdon *n.*
An 'injured' footballer's limp back into the game which draws applause but doesn't fool anybody.

Hodnet *n.*
The wooden safety platform supported by scaffolding round a building under construction from which the builders (at almost no personal risk) can drop pieces of concrete on passers-by.

Hoff *vb.*
To deny indignantly something which is palpably true.

Hoggeston *n.*
The action of overshaking a pair of dice in a cup in the mistaken belief that this will affect the eventual outcome in your favour and not irritate everyone else.

Hordle *vb.*
To dissemble fruitily, in the manner of Donald Sinden.

Horton-cum-Studley *n.*
The combination of little helpful grunts, nodding movements of the head, considerate smiles, upward frowns and serious pauses that a group of people join in making to elicit the next pronouncement of somebody with a terrible stutter.

Hosmer *vb.*
(Of a TV newsreader) To continue to stare impassively into the camera when it should have already switched to the sports report.

Hotagen *n.*
The aggressiveness with which a shop
assistant sells you any piece of high
technology which they don't understand
themselves.

Hove *adj.*
Descriptive of the expression on the face of a
person in the presence of another who clearly
isn't going to stop talking for a very long time.

Huby *n.*
A half-erection large enough to be a publicly
embarrassing bulge in the trousers, but not
large enough to be of any use to anybody.

Hucknall *vb.*
To crouch upwards: as in the movement of a
seated person's feet and legs made to allow
a cleaner's Hoover to pass beneath them.

Hugglescote *n.*
The kind of person who excitedly opens a
letter which says 'You may already have won
£10,000' on the outside.

Hull *adj.*
Descriptive of the smell of a weekend cottage.

Humber *vb.*
To move like the cheeks of a very fat person
as their car goes over a cattle grid.

Humby *n.*
An erection which won't go down when a
gentleman has to go to the lavatory in the
middle of dallying with a lady.

Huna *n.*
The result of coming to the wrong decision.

Hunsingore *n.*
Medieval ceremonial brass horn with which
the successful execution of an araglin (q.v.)
is trumpeted from the castle battlements.

Hutlerburn *n.*
(ARCHAIC) A burn sustained as a result of
the behaviour of a clumsy hutler. (The precise
duties of hutlers are now lost in the mists of
history.)

Huttoft *n.*
The fibrous algae which grow in the dark, moist environment of trouser turn-ups.

Hynish *adj.*
Descriptive of the state of mind in which you might as well give up doing whatever it is you're trying to do because you'll only muck it up.

I

Ible *adj.*
Clever but lazy.

Ibstock *n.*
Anything used to make a noise on a
corrugated-iron wall or clinker-built fence by
dragging it along the surface while walking
past it.
'Mr Bennet thoughtfully selected a stout
ibstock and left the house.' – Jane Austen,
Pride and Prejudice II.

Imber *vb.*
To lean from side to side while watching a car
chase in the cinema.

Inigonish *adj.*
Descriptive of the glassy smile of a dinner
party guest trying to get across both huge
enjoyment to the host, and 'time to go home,
I think' to a partner: failure to notice it will
result in a heanton punchardon (q.v.)

Inverinate *vb.*
To spot that both people in a heated argument
are talking complete rubbish.

Inverkeithing *ptcpl.vb.*
Addressing someone by mumble because
you can only remember the first letter of their
name.

Iping *ptcpl.vb.*
The increasingly anxious shifting from leg to
leg you go through when you are desperate
to go to the lavatory and the person you are
talking to keeps on remembering a few final
things he wants to mention.

Ipplepen *n.*
A useless writing implement made by
Sellotaping six biros together which is
supposed to make it easier to write 100 lines.

Ipswich *n.*
The pregnant whirring at the other end of the phone that precedes a pre-recorded junk call about payment protection insurance.

Islesteps *pl.n.*
Cautious movements towards the bathroom in a strange house in the dark.

J

Jalingo *n.*
The alacrity with which a grimbister (q.v.) breaks up as soon as the police car turns off.

Jarrow *n.*
An agricultural device which, when towed behind a tractor, enables the farmer to spread his dung evenly across the width of the road.

Jawcraig *n.*
(MEDICAL) A massive facial spasm which is brought on by being told a really astounding piece of news.

A mysterious attack of jawcraig affected 40,000 sheep in Wales in 1952.

Jawf *n.*
Conversation between two football hooligans on a train.

Jeffers *pl.n.*
Persons who honestly believe that a business lunch is going to achieve something.

Jid *n.*
The piece of paper on top of the jam inside the jam jar.

Jofane *adj.*
In breach of the laws of joke telling, e.g. giving away the punchline in advance.

Joliette *n.*
(OLD FRENCH) Polite word for a well-proportioned dog-turd.

Joplin *n.*
The material Primark make their clothes from.

Jubones *pl.n.*
Awful things bought in Nairobi which never look good at home.

Jurby *n.*
A loose woollen garment reaching to the knees and with three or more armholes, knitted by the wearer's well-meaning but incompetent aunt.

Juwain *adj.*
Only slightly relevant to the matter in hand.

K

Kabwum *n.*
The cutesy humming noise you make as you go to kiss someone on the cheek.

Kalami *n.*
The ancient Eastern art of being able to fold road maps properly.

Kanturk *n.*
An extremely intricate knot originally used for belaying the topgallant foresheets of a gaff-rigged China clipper, and now more commonly observed when trying to get an old kite out of the cupboard under the stairs.

Keele *n.*
The horrible smell caused by washing ashtrays.

Kelling *ptcpl.vb.*
The action of looking for something all over again in all the places you've already looked.

Kenilworth *n.*
Measure. Defined as that proportion of a menu which the waiter speaks that you can actually remember.

Kent *adj.*
Politely determined not to help despite a violent urge to the contrary.

Kent expressions are seen on the faces of people who are good at something watching someone else who can't do it at all.

Kentucky *adj.*
Fitting exactly and satisfyingly.

The cardboard box that slides neatly into a small space in a garage, or the last book which precisely fills a bookshelf, is said to fit 'real nice and kentucky'.

Kerry *n.*
The small twist of skin which separates each sausage on a string.

Kettering *n.*
The marks left on your bottom or thighs after sunbathing on a wickerwork chair.

Kettleness *adj.*
The quality of not being able to pee while being watched.

Kibblesworth *n.*
The footling amount of money by which a price is less than a sensible number. For example, a flat-screen TV at £1,999.99 has a kibblesworth of 1p.

Kilvaxter *n.*
A pen kept in the desk tidy that never works.

Kimmeridge *n.*
The light breeze which blows through your armpit hair when you are stretched out sunbathing.

Kingston Bagpuise *n.*
A forty-year-old sixteen-stone man trying to commit suicide by jogging.

Kirby *n.*
Small but repulsive piece of food prominently attached to a person's face or clothing.

Kirby Misperton *n.*
One who kindly attempts to wipe a kirby (q.v.)
off another's face with a napkin, and then
discovers it to be a wart or other permanent
fixture, is said to have committed a 'kirby
misperton'.

Kitmurvy *n.*
One who has all the latest gadgetry and
clothing (golf cart, tee cosies, ventilated
shoes, Rory McIlroy autographed top,
American navy cap, mirror sunglasses) but
is still only on his second lesson.

Kittybrewster *n.*
The girl who always offers to make the tea.

Klosters *pl.n.*
The little blobs of dried urine on the rim of
the bowl under the seat.

Knaptoft *n.*
The mysterious fluff placed in your pockets
by dry-cleaning firms.

Kowloon *n.*
One who goes to an Indian restaurant and orders an omelette.

Kurdistan *n.*
Hard stare given by a husband to his wife when he notices a sharp increase in the number of times he answers the phone to be told, 'Sorry, wrong number.'

L

Lackawanna *n.*
The inability of a New York cab driver to know where, for instance, Central Park is.

Lambarene *adj.*
Feeling better for having put pyjamas on.

Lamlash *n.*
The folder on hotel dressing-tables full of astoundingly dull information.

Lampeter *n.*
The fifth member of a foursome.

Lampung *n.*
The daze which follows turning on the light in the middle of the night.

Largoward *n.*
Motorists' name for the kind of pedestrian
who stands beside a main road and waves on
the traffic, as if it's their right of way.

Laxobigging *ptcpl.vb.*
Struggling to extrude an extremely large turd.

Le Touquet *n.*
A mere nothing, an unconsidered trifle,
a negligible amount. *Un touquet* is often
defined as the difference between the cost of
a bottle of gin bought in an off-licence shop
and one bought in a duty-free shop.

Leazes *pl.n.*
Irritating pains that your doctor tells you not
to be so wet about.

Leeming *ptcpl.vb.*
The business of making silly faces at babies.

Lemvig *n.*
A person who can be relied upon to be doing
worse than you.

Libenge *n.*
Crystallized deposits of old cough mixture.

Libode *adj.*
Being undecided about whether or not you feel sexually attracted to someone.

Liff *n.*
A common object or experience for which no word yet exists.

Limassol *n.*
The correct name for one of those little paper umbrellas which come in cocktails with too much pineapple juice in them.

Lindisfarne *adj.*
Descriptive of the pleasant smell of an empty biscuit tin.

Lingle *vb.*
To touch battery terminals with one's tongue.

Liniclate *adj.*
All stiff and achey in the morning and trying to remember why.

Listowel *n.*
The small mat on the bar designed to be more
absorbent than the bar, but not as absorbent
as your elbows.

Little Urswick *n.*
The member of any class who most inclines
the teacher towards the view that capital
punishment should be introduced in schools.

Llanelli *adj.*
Descriptive of the waggling movement of
a person's hands when shaking water from
them or warming up for a piece of workshop
theatre.

Loberia *n.*
Unshakeable belief that your ears stick out.

Lochranza *n.*
The long unaccompanied wail in the middle
of a Scottish folk song where the pipers nip
round the corner for a couple of drinks.

Lolland *n.*
A person with a low threshold of boredom.

Longniddry *n.*
A droplet which persists in running out of your nose.

Lossiemouth *n.*
One of those middle-aged ladies with just a hint of a luxuriant handlebar moustache.

Lostwithiel *n.*
The deep and peaceful sleep you finally fall into two minutes before the alarm goes off.

Louth *n.*
The sort of man who wears loud check jackets, has his own tankard behind the bar and always gets served before you do.

Low Ardwello *n.*
Seductive remark made hopefully in the back of a taxi.

Low Eggborough *n.*
A quiet little unregarded man in glasses who is building a new kind of atomic bomb in his garden shed.

Lower Peover *n.*
Common solution to the problem of a
humby (q.v.).

Lowestoft *n.*
The correct name for 'navel fluff'.

Lowther *vb.*
(Of a large group of people who have been
to the cinema together.) To stand aimlessly
about on the pavement and argue about
whether to go and eat either a Chinese meal
nearby or an Indian meal at a restaurant
which somebody says is very good but isn't
certain where it is, or just go home, or see
if the pub on the corner's still serving food
– until by the time agreement is reached
everything is shut.

Lubcroy *n.*
The telltale little lump in the top of your
swimming trunks which tells you are
going to have to spend half an hour with a
safety pin trying to pull the drawstring
out again.

Lublin *n.*
That bit of somebody's body which their
partner particularly likes.

Ludlow *n.*
A wad of newspaper, folded table-napkin or
lump of cardboard put under a wobbly table
or chair to make it stand up straight.
 It is perhaps not widely known that air-ace
Sir Douglas Bader used to get about on an
enormous pair of ludlows before he had his
artificial legs fitted.

Luffenham *n.*
Feeling you get when the pubs aren't going
to be open for another forty-five minutes
and the luffness (q.v.) is beginning to wear
a bit thin.

Luffness *n.*
Hearty feeling that comes from walking on
the moors with gumboots and cold ears.

Lulworth *n.*
Measure. A lulworth defines the amount of the length, loudness and embarrassment of a statement you make when everyone else in the room unaccountably stops talking at the same moment.

Luppitt *n.*
The piece of leather which hangs off the bottom of your shoe before you can be bothered to get it mended.

Lupridge *n.*
A bubble behind a piece of wallpaper.

Lusby *n.*
The fold of flesh pushing forward over the top of a bra which is too small for the lady inside it.

Luton *n.*
The horseshoe-shaped rug which goes round a lavatory seat.

Lutton Gowts *n.*
The opposite of green fingers – the effortless propensity to cause plant death.

Lybster *n.*
The artificial chuckle in the voice-over at the end of a supposedly funny television commercial.

Lydd *n.*
A lid. A lydd differs from a lid in that it has nothing to be a lid of, is at least eighteen months old, and is sold in Ye Olde Antique Shoppes.

Lydiard Tregoze *n.*
The opposite of a mavis enderby (q.v.). An unrequited early love of your life who inexplicably still causes terrible pangs even though she married a telephone engineer.

Lyminster *n.*
A homosexual vicar.

Lynwilg *n.*
One of those things that pulls the electric cord back into a vacuum cleaner.

M

Maaruig *n.*
The inexpressible horror of waking up
in the morning and remembering you're
Frankie Boyle.

Macroy *n.*
An authoritative, confident opinion based
on one you read in a newspaper.

Maentwrog *n.*
Welsh for 'typo', an ancient word that once
meant something else.

Malaybalay *adj.*
All excited at suddenly remembering a
wonderful piece of gossip that you want to
pass on to somebody.

Malibu *n.*
The height by which the top of a wave
exceeds the height to which you have rolled
up your trousers.

Manitoba *n.*
A re-courtship ritual. The tentative and
reluctant touching of spouses' toes in bed
after a row.

Mankinholes *pl.n.*
The small holes in a loaf of bread which
give rise to the momentary suspicion that
something may have made its home within.

Mapledurham *n.*
A hideous piece of chipboard veneer
furniture bought in a suburban high-street
furniture store and designed to hold exactly a
year's supply of Sunday colour supplements.

Margaretting Tye *n.*
The unexpectedly intimate bond that forms
when two people you have just introduced
decide they like each other better than they
like you.

Margate *n.*
Someone in a uniform whose mission is to make it impossible to get into a building.

Market Deeping *ptcpl.vb.*
Stealing a single piece of fruit from a street stall.

Marlow *n.*
The bottom drawer in the kitchen where your mother keeps her plastic bags.

Marytavy *n.*
A person to whom, under dire injunctions of silence, you tell a secret which you wish to be far more widely known.

Masberry *n.*
The sap of a giant Nigerian tree from which all canteen jams are made.

Massachusetts *pl.n.*
Those items and particles which people who have just blown their noses are searching for when they look into their hankies.

Mavesyn Ridware *n.*
The stuff belonging to a mavis enderby (q.v.)
which keeps turning up in odd corners of your
house.

Mavis Enderby *n.*
The almost-completely-forgotten girlfriend
from your distant past for whom your wife has
a completely irrational jealousy and hatred.

Maynooth *n.*
One who recklessly tells total strangers to
cheer up, it may never happen.

Meadle *vb.*
To blunder around a woman's breasts in a way
which does absolutely nothing for her.

Meath *adj.*
Warm and very slightly clammy.
    Descriptive of the texture of your hands
after you've tried to dry them on a hot-air-
blowing automatic hand-drying machine.

Melbury Bubb *n.*
A TV celebrity who rises to fame by being
extremely camp.

Melcombe Regis *n.*
The name of the style of decoration used in cocktail lounges in mock-Tudor hotels in Surrey.

Melton Constable *n.*
A patent anti-wrinkle cream which policemen wear to keep themselves looking young.

Memphis *n.*
The little bits of yellow fluff which get trapped in the hinge of the windscreen wipers after polishing the car with a new duster.

Memus *n.*
The little trick people use to remind themselves which is left and which is right.

Meuse *n.*
A period of complete silence on the radio, which means that it must be tuned to Radio 3.

Millinocket *n.*
The thing that rattles around inside an aerosol can.

Milwaukee *n.*
The melodious whistling, chanting and
humming tone of the milwaukee can be heard
whenever a public lavatory is entered. It is
the way the occupants of the cubicles have of
telling you there's no lock on their door and
you can't come in.

Mimbridge *n.*
That which two very boring people have in
common which enables you to get away from
them.

Minchinhampton *n.*
The expression on a man's face when he has
just zipped his trousers up without due care
and attention.

Misool *n.*
A mixture of toothpaste and saliva in a
wash-basin.

Moffat *n.*
That part of a coat which is designed to be sat
on by the person next to you on the bus.

Mogumber *n.*
One who goes round complaining they were cleverer ten years ago.

Mointy *n.*
The last little tear before somebody cheers up.

Moisie *adj.*
The condition of one's face after performing cunnilingus.

Molesby *n.*
The kind of family that drives to the seaside and then sits in the car with all the windows closed, reading the *Sunday Express* and wearing sidcups (q.v.).

Monks Toft *n.*
The bundle of hair which is left after a monk has been tonsured, which he keeps tied up with a rubber band and uses for chasing ants away.

Morangie *adj.*
Faintly nervous that a particular post box 'won't work' when posting an important letter.

Motspur *n.*
The fourth wheel of a supermarket trolley
which looks identical to the other three but
renders the trolley completely uncontrollable.

Mugeary *n.*
(MEDICAL) The substance from which the
unpleasant little yellow globules in the
corners of a sleepy person's eyes are made.

Multan *n.*
An infidel who stains his face with walnut
juice in order to enter Mecca or appear in
a sitcom.

Mummelgum *n.*
An unwholesome substance which clings
to the fingers of successful tomb-robbers.

Munderfield *n.*
A meadow selected, whilst driving past, as
being ideal for a picnic which, from a sitting
position, turns out to be full of stubble, dust
and cowpats and almost impossible to enjoy
yourself in.

Munster *n.*

A person who continually brings up the
subject of property prices.

N

Naas *n.*
The winemaking region of Albania where most of the aasleagh (q.v.) comes from.

Nacton *n.*
The 'n' with which cheap advertising copywriters replace the word 'and' (as in 'fish 'n' chips', 'mix 'n' match', 'assault 'n' battery'), in the mistaken belief that it is in some way chummy or endearing.

Nad *n.*
Measure defined as the distance between a driver's outstretched fingertips and the ticket machine in an automatic car park.
  1 nad = 18.4 cm.

Namber *vb.*
To hang around the table being too shy to sit next to the person you really want to.

Nanhoron *n.*
A tiny valve concealed in the inner ear which enables a deaf grandmother to converse quite normally when she feels like it, but which excludes completely anything which sounds like a request to help with laying the table.

Nantucket *n.*
The secret pocket which eats your train ticket.

Nantwich *n.*
A late-night snack, invented by the Earl of Nantwich, which consists of the dampest thing in the fridge. The Earl, who lived in a flat in Clapham, invented the nantwich to avoid having to go shopping.

Naples *pl.n.*
The tiny depressions in a piece of Ryvita.

Naugatuck *n.*
A plastic sachet containing shampoo, Polyfilla, etc., which is impossible to open except by biting off the corners.

Nazeing *ptcpl.vb.*
The rather unconvincing noises of pretended interest which an adult has to make when brought a small dull object for admiration by a child.

Neen Sollars *pl.n.*
Any ensemble of especially unflattering and peculiar garments worn by someone which tells you that they are right at the forefront of fashion.

Nempnett Thrubwell *n.*
The feeling experienced when driving off for the very first time on a brand new motorbike.

Nindigully *n.*
One who constantly needs to be re-persuaded of something they've already agreed to.

Nipishish *adj.*
Descriptive of a person walking barefoot on gravel.

Nith *n.*
The dark piece of velvet which has been
brushed against the nap.

Noak Hoak *n.*
A driver who indicates left and turns right.

Nogdam End *n.*
That part of a pair of scissors used to bang
in a picture hook.

Nokomis *n.*
One who dresses like an ethnic minority to
which they do not belong.

Nome *sfx.*
Latin suffix meaning: question expecting the
answer, 'Oh really? How interesting.'

Nossob *n.*
Any word that looks as if it's probably another
word backwards but turns out not to be.

Nottage *n.*
The collective name for things which you find
a use for immediately after you have thrown
them away.

For instance, your greenhouse has been
cluttered up for years with a huge piece of
cardboard and great fronds of gardening
string. You at last decide to clear all this stuff
out, and you burn it. Within twenty-four hours
you will urgently need to wrap a large parcel,
and suddenly remember that luckily in your
greenhouse there is some cardb . . .

Nubbock *n.*
The kind of person who has to leave before
a party can relax and enjoy itself.

Nuncargate *adj.*
Able to go on a two-week holiday with hardly
any luggage.

Nundle *vb.*
To move a piano.

Nupend *n.*
The amount of small change found in the
lining of an old jacket which just saves your
bacon.

Nutbourne *n.*
In a choice between two or more possible
puddings, the one nobody plumps for.

Nyarling *ptcpl.vb.*
Of married couples, using a term of
endearment as a term of censure or reproach.

Nybster *n.*
The sort of person who takes the lift to travel
one floor.

O

Ocilla *n.*
The cute little circle or heart over an 'I' used by teenage girls when writing their names.

Ockle *n.*
An electrical switch which appears to be off in both positions.

Offleyhoo *adj.*
Ridiculously over-enthusiastic about going to Cornwall.

Offord Darcy *n.*
A gatecrasher you can't get rid of because he's become the life and soul of the party.

Old Cassop *n.*
Piece of caring reassurance which all parties know is completely untrue. As in 'a load of . . . '

Ompton *n.*
One who has been completely kitted out at
Burberry's but is still, nevertheless, clearly
from Idaho.

Osbaston *n.*
A point made for the seventh time to
somebody who insists that they know exactly
what you mean but clearly hasn't got the
faintest idea.

Oshkosh *n.*
The noise made by someone who has just
been grossly flattered and is trying to make
light of it.

Ospringe *n.*
That part of a three-colour biro which renders
it instantly useless.

Ossett *n.*
A frilly spare-toilet-roll cosy.

Ossining *ptcpl.vb.*
Trying to see past the person sitting in front
of you at the cinema.

Oswaldtwistle *n.*
(OLD NORSE) Small brass wind instrument
used for summoning Vikings to lunch when
they're off on their longships, playing.

Oswestry *adj.*
Unable to find a comfortable position in bed.

Oughterby *n.*
Someone you don't want to invite to a party but
whom you know you have to as a matter of duty.

Oundle *vb.*
To walk along leaning sideways, with one arm
hanging limp and dragging one leg behind the
other.
　　Most commonly used by actors in amateur
productions of *Richard III*, or by people
carrying a heavy suitcase in one hand.

Oystermouth *n.*
One who can kiss and chew gum at the same
time.

Ozark *n.*
One who offers to help after all the work has
been done.

P

Pabbay *n.*
(FENCING) The play, or manoeuvre, where one swordsman leaps on to the table and pulls the battleaxe off the wall.

Pant-y-Wacco *adj.*
The final state of mind of a retired colonel before they come to take him away.

Pantperthog *n.*
An actor whose only talent is to stay fat.

Papcastle *n.*
Something drawn or modelled by a small child that's going to make them very unhappy when you don't know what it's meant to be.

Papigochic *n.*
A middle-aged man's overlong haircut, intended to make him look younger.

Papple *vb.*
To do what babies do to soup with their spoons.

Papworth Everard *n.*
Technical term for the fifth take of an orgasm scene during the making of a pornographic film.

Paradip *n.*
Polite word for the act of washing one's genitals in the wash-basin.

Parbold *adj.*
Nearly brave enough to dive into a cold swimming pool on a windy day.

Parrog *n.*
God knows. Could be some sort of bird, I suppose.

Pathstruie *adj.*
The condition of a parish church after a heavy Saturday afternoon's wedlock.

Patkai Bum *n.*
Mysterious illness afflicting recently deposed
heads of state which means they aren't well
enough to stand trial.

Patney *n.*
Something your next door neighbour makes
and insists that you try on your sausages.

Peebles *pl.n.*
Small, carefully rolled pellets of skegness (q.v.).

Peening Quarter *n.*
That area of a discotheque where single men
lounge about trying to look groovy about not
having the courage to ask a girl to dance.

Pelutho *n.*
A South American ball game. The balls are
whacked against a brick wall with a stout
wooden bat until the prisoner confesses.

Pentre-tafarn-y-fedw *n.*
Welsh word which literally translates as
'leaking-biro-by-the-glass-hole-of-the-clerk-
of-the-bank-has-been-taken-to-another-place-
leaving-only-the-special-inkwell-and-three-
inches-of-tin-chain'.

Penge *n.*
The expanding slotted arm on which a cuckoo
comes out of a cuckoo clock.

Peoria *n.*
The fear of peeling too few potatoes.

Percyhorner *n.*
(ENGLISH PUBLIC-SCHOOL SLANG) A prefect
whose duty it is to surprise new boys at the
urinal and humiliate them in a manner of his
choosing.

Perranzabuloe *n.*
The squirty function in an electric iron.

Peru *n.*
The expression of innocent alarm seen on
the face of someone guiltily surprised in the
middle of a perusal.

Peterculter *n.*
Someone you don't want to be friends with
who rings you up at eight-monthly intervals
and suggests you get together soon.

Pevensey *n.*
(ARCHAIC) The right to collect shingle from
the king's foreshore.

Phillack *n.*
A Gucci belt pouch for carrying condoms in.

Pibsbury *n.*
The little hole in the end of a toothbrush.

Picklenash *n.*
The detritus found in wine glasses on the
morning after a party.

Piddletrenthide *n.*
A trouser stain caused by a wimbledon (q.v.).
Not to be confused with a botley (q.v.).

Pidney *n.*
The amount of coffee in the bottom of the jar
which doesn't amount to a spoonful.

Pimlico *n.*
Small odd-shaped piece of plastic or curious
metal component found in the bottom of
a kitchen rummage-drawer when spring-
cleaning or looking for Sellotape.

Pimperne *n.*
One of those rubber nodules found on the
underneath side of a lavatory seat.

Pingandy *n.*
An extremely neat old person.

Pingaring *n.*
That part of an oven that nobody wants or
knows how to turn off.

Pitlochry *n.*
The background gurgling noise heard in fast
food restaurants caused by people trying to
get the last bubbles out of their milkshakes
by slurping loudly through their straws.

Pitroddie *n.*
A middle- or upper-class person who affects
a working-class style of speech.

Pitsligo *n.*
Part of a traditional mating rite.

During the first hot day of spring, all the
men in the tube start giving up their seats
to ladies and strap-hanging. The purpose of
pitsligo is to allow them to demonstrate their
manhood by displaying the wet patches under
their arms.

Pleeley *adj.*
Descriptive of a drunk person's attempts to
be endearing.

Plenmeller *n.*
The non-waterproof material from which
raincoats are made.

Pleven *n.*
One more, or one less, than the number
required.

Plumgarths *pl.n*
The corrugations on the ankles caused by
wearing tight socks.

Pluvigner *n.*
The minuscule hole in the side of a biro.

Plymouth *vb.*
To relate an amusing story to someone without remembering that it was they who told it to you in the first place.

Plympton *n.*
The knob on top of a war memorial.

Pocking *n.*
The pointless tapping of a cigarette before getting on with the business of smoking it.

Podebrady *n.*
The man in dirty overalls hired to wander whistling round the corridors of a large corporation to make it look as if the management's getting something done.

Pode Hole *n.*
An aperture in a lavatory wall used for a number of purposes.

Pofadder *n.*
A snake that can't be bothered to bite you.

Poffley End *n.*
The green bit of a carrot.

Poges *pl.n.*
The lumps of dry powder that remain after
cooking a packet of soup.

Polbathic *adj.*
Gifted with the ability to manipulate taps
using only the feet.

Pollatomish *adj.*
Peevish, restless, inclined to pull the stuffing
out of sofas.

Polloch *n.*
One of those tiny ribbed-plastic and
aluminium foil tubs of milk served on trains
enabling you to carry one safely back to your
compartment where you can spill the contents
all over your legs in comfort trying to get the
bloody thing open.

Polperro *n.*
The ball, or muff, of soggy hair found clinging
to bath overflow-holes.

Polyphant *n.*
The mythical beast – part bird, part snake, part jam stain – which invariably wins children's painting competitions in the 5–7 age group.

Pontybodkin *n.*
The stance adopted by a seaside comedian which tells you that the punchline is imminent.

Poona *n.*
Satisfied grunting noise made when sitting back after a good meal.

Potarch *n.*
The eldest male in a soap opera family.

Pott Shrigley *n.*
Dried remains of a week-old casserole, eaten when extremely drunk at two a.m.

Prague *vb.*
To declaim loudly and pompously upon any subject about which the speaker has less knowledge than at least one other person at the table.

Preston Gubbals *n.*
Breasts of uneven weight.

Princes Risborough *n.*
The right of any member of the Royal Family
to have people laugh at their jokes, however
weedy.

Prungle *adj.*
Pretending to be proud to be single.

Pudsey *n.*
The curious-shaped flat wads of dough left
on a kitchen table after someone has been
cutting scones out of it.

Pulverbatch *n.*
The first paragraph on the blurb of a dust-
jacket in which famous authors claim to have
had a series of menial jobs in their youth.

Puning *ptcpl.vb.*
Boosting a man's ego by pretending to be
unable to open a screwtop jar.

Pymble *n.*
Small metal object about the size of a thimble
which lies on the ground. When you kick it
you discover it is the top of something buried
four feet deep.

Q

Quabbs *pl.n.*
The substances which emerge when you
squeeze a blackhead.

Quall *vb.*
To speak with the voice of one who requires
another to do something for them.

Quedgeley *n.*
A rabidly left-wing politician who can
afford to be that way because he married a
millionairess.

Quenby *n.*
A stubborn spot on a window which you
spend twenty minutes trying to clean off
before discovering it's on the other side of
the glass.

Querrin *n.*
A person that no one has ever heard of who unaccountably manages to make a living writing prefaces.

Quoyness *n.*
The hatefulness of words like 'relionus' and 'easiphit'.

R

Radlett *n.*
The single hemisphere of dried pea which is invariably found in an otherwise spotlessly clean saucepan.

Ramsgate *n.*
All institutional buildings must, by law, contain at least twenty ramsgates. These are doors which open the opposite way to the one you expect.

Randers *pl.n.*
People who, for their own obscure reasons, try to sleep with people who have slept with members of the Royal Family.

Ranfurly *adj.*
Fashion of tying ties so that the long thin end dangles below the short fat end.

Ravenna *n.*
Poetic term for the cleavage in a workman's bottom that peeks above the top of his trousers.

Reculver *n.*
The sort of remark only ever made on *Any Questions*.

Rhymney *n.*
That part of a song lyric which you suddenly discover you've been mishearing for years.

Riber *n.*
The barely soiled sheet of toilet paper which signals the end of the bottom-wiping process.

Richmond *adj.*
Descriptive of the state that very respectable elderly ladies get into if they have a little too much sherry, which, as everyone knows, does not make you drunk.

Rickling *ptcpl.vb.*
Fiddling around inside a magazine to remove all the stapled-in special offer cards that make it impossible to read.

Rigolet *n.*
As much of an opera as most people can sit
through.

Rimbey *n.*
The particularly impressive throw of a frisbee
which causes it to be lost.

Ripon *vb.*
(Of literary critics) To include all the best
jokes from the book in the review to make it
look as if the critic thought of them.

Risplith *n.*
The burst of applause which greets the sound
of a plate smashing in a canteen.

Rochester *n.*
One who is able to gain occupation of the
armrests on both sides of their cinema or
aircraft seat.

Roosebeck *n.*
Useful all-purpose emergency word. When
a child asks, 'Daddy, what's that bird/flower/
funny thing that man's wearing?' you simply
reply, 'It's a roosebeck, darling.'

Royston *n.*
The man behind you in church who sings with terrific gusto almost three-quarters of a tone off the note.

Rudge *n.*
An unjust criticism of your ex-girlfriend's new boyfriend.

Rufforth *n.*
One who has the strength of character or loudness of voice to bring a lowthering (q.v.) session to an end.

S

Sadberge *n.*
A violent-green shrub which is ground up,
mixed with twigs and gelatine and served
with clonmult (q.v.) and buldoo (q.v.) in a
container referred to for no known reason as
the 'relish tray'.

Saffron Walden *n.*
A loud sports jacket that nobody wears in
real life but is never out of fashion on *The
Two Ronnies*.

Salween *n.*
A faint taste of washing-up liquid in a cup
of tea.

Samalaman *n.*
One who fills in the gaps in conversations by
beaming genially at people and saying, 'Well,
well, well, here we all are then', a lot.

Satterthwaite *vb.*
To spray the person you are talking to with half-chewed breadcrumbs or small pieces of whitebait.

Saucillo *n.*
A joke told by someone who completely misjudges the temperament of the person to whom it is told.

Savernake *vb.*
To sew municipal crests on to an anorak in the belief that this makes the wearer appear cosmopolitan.

Scackleton *n.*
Horizontal avalanche of CDs that slides across the interior of a car as it goes round a sharp corner.

Scamblesby *n.*
A small dog which resembles a throw-rug and appears to be dead.

Scethrog *n.*
One of those peculiar beards-without-moustaches worn by religious Belgians and American scientists which help them look like trolls.

Sconser *n.*
A person who looks around them when talking to you, to see if there's anyone more interesting about.

Scopwick *n.*
The flap of skin which is torn off your lip when trying to smoke an untipped cigarette.

Scorrier *n.*
A small hunting dog trained to snuffle amongst your private parts.

Scosthrop *vb.*
To make vague opening or cutting movements with the hands when wandering about looking for a tin opener, scissors, etc., in the hope that this will help in some way.

Scrabby *n.*
A curious-shaped duster given to you by your
mother which on closer inspection turns out
to be half an underpant.

Scrabster *n.*
One of those dogs which has it off on your leg
during tea.

Scramoge *vb.*
To cut oneself whilst licking envelopes.

Scranton *n.*
A person who, after the declaration of the
bodmin (q.v.), always says, '. . . But I only had
the tomato soup.'

Scraptoft *n.*
The absurd flap of hair a vain and balding
man grows long above one ear to comb it
plastered over the top of his head to the other
ear.

Screeb *vb.*
To make the noise of a nylon anorak rubbing
against a pair of corduroy trousers.

Screggan *n.*
(BANKING) The crossed-out bit caused by
people putting the wrong year on their
cheques all through January.

Scremby *n.*
The dehydrated felt-tip pen attached by
a string to the 'Don't Forget' board in the
kitchen which has never worked in living
memory but which no one can be bothered
to throw away.

Scridain *n.*
The look bestowed on the human race by
Jeremy Paxman.

Scroggs *pl.n.*
The stout pubic hairs which protrude from
your helping of moussaka in a cheap Greek
restaurant.

Scronkey *n.*
Something that hits the window as a result
of a violent sneeze.

Scugog *n.*
One whose mouth actually hangs open when watching something mildly interesting on the other side of the street.

Scullet *n.*
The last teaspoon in the washing up.

Scurlage *n.*
A duck-web of snot caused by sneezing into your hand.

Seattle *vb.*
To make a noise like a train going along.

Shalunt *n.*
One who wears Trinidad and Tobago T-shirts on the beach in Bali to prove they didn't just win the holiday in a competition or anything.

Shanklin *n.*
The hoop of skin around a single slice of salami.

Sheepy Magna *n.*
One who emerges unexpectedly from the wrong bedroom in the morning.

Sheppey *n.*
Measure of distance (equal to approximately seven-eighths of a mile), defined as the closest distance at which sheep remain picturesque.

Shifnal *n.*
An awkward shuffling walk caused by two or more people in a hurry accidentally getting in the same segment of a revolving door.

Shimpling *ptcpl.vb.*
Lying about the state of your life in order to cheer up your parents.

Shirmers *pl.n.*
Tall young men who stand around smiling at weddings as if to suggest that they know the bride rather well.

Shoeburyness *n.*
The vague uncomfortable feeling you get when sitting on a seat which is still warm from somebody else's bottom.

Shottle *n.*
One of those tubes made of yellow plastic
dustbins which builders use to get rubble off
the top floor of a house.

Shrenk *n.*
A fold in a pair of stockings that aren't tight
enough for a pair of thin legs.

Shrivenham *n.*
One of Germaine Greer's used-up lovers.

Sicamous *adj.*
Perfectly willing to appear on *The Alan
Titchmarsh Show*.

Sidcup *n.*
A hat made from tying knots in the corners
of a handkerchief.

Sigglesthorne *n.*
Anything used in lieu of a toothpick.

Silesia *n.*
(MEDICAL) The inability to remember, at the
critical moment, which is the better side of
the boat to be seasick off.

Silloth *n.*
Something that was sticky, and is now furry,
found on the carpet under the sofa on the
morning after a party.

Simprim *n.*
The little movement of false modesty by
which a woman with a cavernous visible
cleavage pulls her skirt down over her knees.

Sittingbourne *n.*
One of those conversations where both people
are waiting for the other one to shut up so
they can get on with their bit.

Skagway *n.*
Sudden outbreak of cones on a motorway.

Skannerup *n.*
A Swedish casserole made of elk-livers.

Skegness *n.*
Nose excreta of a malleable consistency.

Skellister *n.*
A very, very old solicitor.

Skellow *adj.*
Descriptive of the satisfaction experienced
when looking at a really good drystone wall.

Skenfrith *n.*
The flakes of athlete's foot found inside socks.

Sketty *n.*
Apparently self-propelled little dance a beer
glass performs in its own puddle.

Skibbereen *n.*
The noise made by a sunburned thigh leaving
a plastic chair.

Skoonspruit *n.*
The tiny garden sprinkler thing your mouth
sometimes does for no apparent reason.

Skrubburdnut *n.*
One who draws penises on posters of women
in the Underground.

Skulamus *n.*
Someone who is obviously not doing what
they went into the lavatory for.

Slabberts *pl.n.*
People who say, 'Can I have some more juice?' when they mean gravy.

Slettnut *n.*
Something which goes round and round but won't come off.

Slipchitsy *n.*
Someone who takes the morning off work in order to sign on.

Slobozia *n.*
A chronic inability to pick up underpants.

Slogarie *n.*
Hillwalking dialect for the stretch of concealed rough moorland which lies between what you thought was the top of the hill and what actually is.

Sloinge *n.*
A post self-abuse tristesse.

Sloothby *adj.*
Conspicuously inconspicuous – as of a major celebrity entering a restaurant with a great display of being incognito.

Slubbery *n.*
The gooey drips of wax that dribble down the sides of a candle.

Sluggan *n.*
A lurid facial bruise which everybody politely omits to mention because it's obvious that you had a punch-up with your spouse last night – but which was actually caused by walking into a door. It is useless to volunteer the true explanation because nobody will believe it.

Slumbay *n.*
The cigarette end someone discovers in the mouthful of lager they have just swigged from a can at the end of a party.

Smarden *vb.*
To keep your mouth shut by smiling
determinedly through your teeth.
    Smardening is largely used by people
trying to give the impression that they're
enjoying a story they've heard at least six
times before.

Smearisary *n.*
The part of a kitchen wall reserved for the
schooltime daubings of small children.

Smisby *n.*
The correct name for a junior apprentice
greengrocer whose main duty is to arrange the
fruit so that the bad side is underneath.
    From the name of a character not in
Dickens.

Smyrna *n.*
The expression on the face of one whose joke
has gone down rather well.

Sneem *n.*
Particular kind of frozen smile bestowed on
a small child by a parent in mixed company
when the question, 'Mummy, what's this?'
appears to require the answer, 'Er . . . it's a
rubber johnny, darling.'

Snitter *n.*
One of the rather unfunny newspaper
clippings pinned to an office wall, the humour
of which is supposed to derive from the fact
that the headline contains a name similar to
that of one of the occupants of the office.

Snitterby *n.*
Someone who pins up snitters (q.v.).

Snitterfield *n.*
Office noticeboard on which snitters (q.v.),
cards saying 'You don't have to be mad to
work here, but if you are, it helps!!!' and
smutty postcards from Ibiza get pinned up
by snitterbies (q.v.).

Snoul *n.*
The third recurrence of a winter cold.

Snover *n.*
One who is reduced to drinking coffee from his egg-cups in order to put off the washing up just one more week.

Solent *adj.*
Descriptive of the state of serene self-knowledge reached through drink.

Soller *vb.*
To break something in two while testing if you glued it together properly.

Sompting *n.*
The practice of dribbling involuntarily into one's own pillow.

Sotterley *n.*
Uncovered bit between two shops with awnings, which you have to cross when it's raining.

Southwick *n.*
A left-handed wanker.

Spiddle *vb.*
To fritter away a perfectly good life
pretending to develop film projects.

Spinwam *n.*
The toxic foam that clings to rocky foreshores.

Spittal of Glenshee *n.*
That which has to be cleaned off castle
doors in the morning after a bagpipe-playing
contest or vampire attack.

Spoffard *n.*
An MP whose contribution to politics is
limited to saying 'Hear, Hear'.

Spofforth *vb.*
To tidy up a room before the cleaning lady
arrives.

Spokane *vb.*
To remove precious objects from a room
before a party.

Spreakley *adj.*
Irritatingly cheerful in the morning.

Spruce Knob *n.*
A genital aftershave which is supposed to be
catching on in America.

Spurger *n.*
One who in answer to the question 'How are
you?' actually tells you.

Spuzzum *n.*
A wee-wee which resembles a lawn sprinkler,
caused by a shred of tissue paper covering
the exit hole of the penis.

Squibnocket *n.*
That part of a car, the unexpected need for
the replacement of which causes garage bills
to be four times larger than the estimate.

Stagno di Gumbi *n.*
(ITALIAN) Pissed off with waiting for a bus to
arrive, a waiter to bring the menu, or a genius
to finish painting your ceiling.

Staplow *n.*
A telephone number that you now can't find
anywhere because two years ago you swore
you would never speak to the person again.

Stebbing *n.*
The erection you cannot conceal because you are not wearing a jacket.

Steenhuffel *n.*
One who is employed by a trade delegation or negotiating team to swell the numbers and make it look impressive when they walk out. There are currently 25,368 steenhuffels working at the UN in New York.

Stelling Minnis *n.*
A traditional street dance. This lovely old gigue can be seen at any time of the year in the streets of the City of London or the Courts of the Old Bailey. Wherever you see otherwise perfectly staid groups of bankers, barristers or ordinary members of the public moving along in a slightly syncopated way you may be sure that a stelling minnis is taking place. The phenomenon is caused by the fact that the dancers are trying not to step on the cracks in the pavement in case the bears get them.

Stibb *n.*
An unwelcome poke in the ribs by someone
who hardly knows you.

'Mr Gervais stibbed Her Royal Highness
repeatedly with his huby' (q.v.). *The Times*

Stibbard *n.*
The invisible brake pedal on the passenger's
side of the car.

Stody *n.*
A small drink which someone nurses for
hours so they can stay in the pub.

Stoke Poges *n.*
The tapping movements of an index finger on
glass made by a person futilely attempting to
communicate with either a tropical fish or a
Post Office clerk.

Stowting *ptcpl.vb.*
Feeling a pregnant woman's tummy.

Strassgang *n.*
German word for the group of workers hired
to lunch inside a string of motorway cones, or
skagway (q.v.).

Strelley *n.*
Long strip of paper or tape which has got
tangled round the wheel of something.

Strubby *adj.*
Attractively miniature.

Sturry *n.*
A token run. Pedestrians who have chosen
to cross a road immediately in front of an
approaching vehicle generally give a little
wave and break into a sturry. This gives the
impression of hurrying without having any
practical effect on their speed whatsoever.

Stutton *n.*
Tiny melted plastic nodule which fails to help
fasten a duvet cover.

Suckley Knowl *n.*
A plumber's assistant who never knows where
the actual plumber is.

Surby *adj.*
Insolently polite, as of policemen who have stopped a motorist.

Sutton and Cheam *ns.*
Sutton and Cheam are the two kinds of dirt into which all dirt is divided. 'Sutton' is the dark sort that always gets on to light-coloured things, and 'cheam' the light-coloured sort that always clings on to dark items. Anyone who has ever found Marmite stains on a dress-shirt, or seagull goo on a dinner jacket a) knows all about sutton and cheam, and b) is going to some very curious dinner parties.

Swaffham Bulbeck *n.*
An entire picnic lunchtime spent fighting off wasps.

Swanage *n.*
The diversionary tactics used when trying
to cover up the existence of a glossop (q.v.).
May include (a) uttering a high-pitched
laugh and pointing out of the window (this
doesn't work more than twice); (b) sneezing
as loudly as possible, whipping out your
handkerchief and swiping the glossop from
the table in the same movement; (c) saying,
'Christ! I seem to have dropped some shit
on your table' (unwise); (d) saying, 'Jesus,
who did that?' (better); (e) pressing your
elbow onto the glossop and working your arm
slowly to the edge of the table; (f) leaving the
glossop where it is but moving a plate over
it and putting up with sitting at an awkward
angle for the rest of the meal; or (g) if the
glossop is in too exposed a position, leaving
it there unremarked except for the occasional
humorous glance.

Swanibost *adj.*
Completely shagged out after a hard day
having income tax explained to you.

Swefling *ptcpl.vb.*
Using a special attachment to Hoover a sofa.

Symonds Yat *n.*
The little spoonful inside the lid of a recently opened boiled egg.

T

Tabley Superior *n.*
The look directed at you in a theatre bar
during the interval by people who've already
got their drinks.

Tampa *n.*
The sound of a rubber eraser coming to rest
after dropping off a desk in a very quiet room.

Tananarive *vb.*
To announce your entrance by falling over the
dustbin in the drive.

Tanvats *pl.n.*
Disturbing things that the previous owners of
your house have left in the cellar.

Tarabulus *n.*
The geometrical figure which describes the
Ban the Bomb sign or a car steering wheel.

Taroom *vb.*
To make loud noises during the night to let the burglars know you are in.

Teigngrace *n.*
The belief that a Devon cream tea is not going to make you feel sick after you've eaten it.

Tew *n.*
Tuft of hair that grows between a man's eyebrows.

Tewel *n.*
The little brass latch which fastens the front wall of a doll's house.

Throcking *ptcpl.vb.*
The action of continually pushing down the lever on a pop-up toaster in the hope that you will thereby get it to understand that you want it to toast something.

Throckmorton *n.*
The soul of a departed madman: one of those now known to inhabit the timing mechanisms of pop-up toasters.

Thrumster *n.*
The irritating man next to you in a concert
who thinks he's the conductor.

Thrupp *vb.*
To hold a ruler on one end of a desk and
make the other end go bbddbbddbbrrbrrrddrr.

Thurnby *n.*
A rucked-up edge of carpet or linoleum which
everyone says someone will trip over and
break a leg unless it gets fixed. After a year or
two someone trips over it and breaks a leg.

Tibshelf *n.*
Criss-cross wooden construction hung on
a wall in a teenage girl's bedroom which
is covered with glass Bambis and poodles,
matching pigs and porcelain ponies in
various postures.

Tidpit *n.*
The corner of a toenail from which satisfying
little black spots may be sprung.

Tigharry *n.*
The accomplice who lures punters to participate in the three-card trick by winning an improbable amount of money very easily.

Tillicoultry *n.*
The man-to-man chumminess adopted by an employer as a prelude to telling an employee that he's going to have to let him go.

Timble *vb.*
(Of small nasty children) To fall over very gently, look around to see who's about, and then yell blue murder.

Tincleton *n.*
A man who amuses himself in your lavatory by pulling the chain in mid-pee and then seeing if he can finish before the flush does.

Tingewick *n.*
The first, sleepy morning stirrings of the penis.

Tingrith *n.*
The feeling of silver paper against your fillings.

Tockholes *pl.n.*
The tiny meaningless perforations which
infest brogues.

Todber *n.*
One whose idea of a good time is to stand
behind his front hedge and give surly nods to
people he doesn't know.

Todding *ptcpl.vb.*
The business of talking amicably and
aimlessly to the barman at the local.

Tolob *n.*
The crease or fold in an underblanket the
removal of which involves getting out of bed
and largely remaking it.

Tolstachaolais *phr.*
What the police in Leith require you to say in
order to prove that you are not drunk.

Tomatin *n.*
The chemical from which tinned tomato soup
is made.

Tonypandy *n.*
The voice used by presenters on children's
television programmes.

Toodyay *n.*
Indonesian expression meaning 'sometime
next month'.

Tooting Bec *n.*
A car behind which one draws up at the
traffic lights and hoots at when the lights go
green before realizing that the car is parked
and there is no one inside.

Torlundy *n.*
Narrow but thickly grimed strip of floor
between the fridge and the sink unit in the
kitchen of a rented flat.

Toronto *n.*
Generic term for anything which comes out
in a gush despite all your careful efforts to
let it out gently, e.g. flour into a white sauce,
tomato ketchup on to fried fish, sperm into a
human being, etc.

Totteridge *n.*
The ridiculous two-inch hunch that people adopt when arriving late for the theatre in the vain hope that it will minimize either the embarrassment or the lack of visibility for the rest of the audience.

Trantlemore *vb.*
To make a noise like a train crossing a set of points.

Trewoofe *n.*
A very thick and heavy drift of snow balanced precariously on the edge of a door porch awaiting for what it judges to be the correct moment to fall.

   From the ancient Greek legend 'The Trewoofe of Damocles'.

Trispen *n.*
A form of intelligent grass. It grows a single, tough stalk and makes its home on lawns. When it sees the lawnmower coming it lies down and pops up again after it has gone by.

Trossachs *pl.n.*
The useless epaulettes on an expensive
raincoat.

Trunch *n.*
Instinctive resentment of people younger
than you.

Tuamgraney *n.*
A hideous wooden ornament that people
hang over the mantelpiece to prove they've
been to Africa.

Tukituki *n.*
A sexual liaison which is meant to be secret
but which is in fact common knowledge.

Tullynessle *n.*
An honest attempt to track down a clitoris.

Tulsa *n.*
A slurp of beer which has accidentally gone
down your shirt collar.

Tumby *n.*
The involuntary abdominal gurgling which
fills the silence following someone else's
intimate personal revelation.

Tweedsmuir *collective n.*
The name given to the extensive collection
of hats kept in the downstairs lavatory which
don't fit anyone in the family.

Twomileborris *n.*
A popular East European outdoor game in
which the first person to reach the front of
the meat queue wins, and the losers have to
forfeit their bath plugs.

U

Udine *adj.*
Not susceptible to charm.

Ugglebarnby *n.*
The ponytail affected by a middle-aged
balding man.

Ullapool *n.*
The spittle which builds up on the floor of
the orchestra pit of the Royal Opera House.

Ullingswick *n.*
An over-developed epiglottis found in
middle-aged coloraturas.

Ullock *n.*
The correct name for either of the deaf
Scandinavian tourists two abreast in front
of you on the escalator.

Ulting *ptcpl.vb.*
Clicking the jaw to unpop the ears.

Umberleigh *n.*
The awful moment which follows a dorchester
(q.v.) when a speaker weighs up whether
to repeat an amusing remark after nobody
laughed the last time. To be on the horns of
an umberleigh is to wonder whether people
didn't hear the remark, or whether they did
hear it and just didn't think it was funny,
which was why somebody coughed.

Upottery *n.*
That part of a kitchen cupboard which
contains an unnecessarily large number of
milk jugs.

Urchfont *n.*
Sudden stab of hypocrisy which goes through
the mind when taking vows as a godparent.

Uttoxeter *n.*
A small but immensely complex mechanical
device which is essentially the 'brain' of a
modern coffee machine, and which enables
the machine to take its own decisions.

V

Valletta *n.*
An ornate head-dress or loose garment worn
by a person in the belief that it renders them
invisibly native and not like tourists at all.
People who don huge conical straw coolie
hats with 'I luv Lagos' on them in Nigeria,
or fat solicitors from Tonbridge on holiday in
Malaya who insist on appearing in the hotel
lobby wearing a sarong know what we are
on about.

Vancouver *n.*
The technical name for one of those huge
trucks with whirling brushes on the bottom
used to clean streets.

Ventnor *n.*
One who, having been visited as a child by
a mysterious gypsy lady, is gifted with the
strange power of being able to operate the
air-nozzles above aeroplane seats.

Vidlin *n.*

The moistly frayed end of a piece of cotton thread.

'It is easier for a rich man to enter the Kingdom of Heaven than it is for a vidlin to pass through the eye of a needle.'

Visby *n.*

The pointy, tent-like structure in the bedclothes with which a man indicates to his partner that he thinks it's high time she stopped fiddling around in the bathroom cupboard and came to bed.

Vollenhove *n.*

One who indicates from thirty yards across a crowded street that they have spotted you, wish to speak with you, and that you are required to remain rooted to the spot waiting for them.

W

Waccamaw *n.*
An exotic Brazilian bird which makes
its home in the audiences of BBC Light
Entertainment radio shows and screeches
when it hears the word 'bottom'.

Warleggan *n.*
(ARCHAIC) One who does not approve of
araglins (q.v.).

Wartnaby *n.*
Something you only discover about somebody
the first time they take their clothes off in
front of you.

Wasp Green *adj.*
The paint in the catalogue which is quite
obviously yellow.

Watendlath *n.*
The bit of wood a cabbie removes so as to
open his sliding window and give you the full
benefit of his opinions.

Wawne *n.*
A badly suppressed yawn.

Wedderlairs *pl.n*
The large patches of sweat on the back of a
hot man's T-shirt.

Wembley *n.*
The hideous moment of confirmation that the
disaster presaged in the ely (q.v.) has actually
struck.

Wendens Ambo *n.*
(VETERINARY) The circuitous digestive system
of a cow; hence also, a futile attempt to enter
or exit Swindon by road.

West Wittering *ptcpl.vb.*
The uncontrollable twitching which breaks
out when you're trying to get away from the
most boring person at a party.

Wetwang *n.*
A moist penis.

Whaplode Drove *n.*
A homicidal golf stroke.

Whasset *n.*
A business card in your wallet belonging
to someone whom you have no recollection
of meeting.

Whissendine *n.*
A noise which occurs (often by night) in a
strange house, which is too short and too
irregular for you ever to be able to find out
what it is and where it comes from.

Widdicombe *n.*
(ARCHAIC) The sort of person who
impersonates Trimphones.

Wigan *n.*
If, when talking to someone you know has
only one leg, you're trying to treat them
perfectly casually and normally, but find to
your horror that your conversation is liberally
studded with references to (a) Long John
Silver, (b) Hopalong Cassidy, (c) the Hokey
Cokey, (d) 'putting your foot in it', (e) 'the last
leg of the UEFA competition', you are said to
have committed a wigan.

Wike *vb.*
To rip a piece of sticky plaster off your skin
as fast as possible in the hope that it will
(a) show how brave you are and (b) not hurt.

Willimantic *adj.*
Of a person whose heart is in the wrong place
(i.e. between their legs).

Wimbledon *n.*
The last drop which, no matter how much you
shake it, always goes down your trouser leg.

Winkley *n.*
A lost object which turns up immediately
you've gone and bought a replacement for it.

Winster *n.*
One who is mistakenly under the impression
that they are charming.

Winston-Salem *n.*
A person in a restaurant who suggests to their
companions that they should split the cost of
a meal equally, and then orders two packets
of cigarettes on the bill.

Wivenhoe *n.*
The cry of alacrity with which a sprightly
eighty-year-old breaks the ice on the lake
when going for a swim on Christmas Eve.

Woking *ptcpl.vb.*
Standing in the kitchen wondering what you
came in here for.

Wollondilly *n.*
A woman who can't get her lipstick on
straight.

Worgret *n.*
A kind of poltergeist which specializes in
stealing new copies of the *A–Z* from your car.

Worksop *n.*
A person who never actually gets round to doing anything because he spends all his time writing out lists headed 'Things To Do (Urgent)'.

Wormelow Tump *n.*
Any seventeen-year-old who doesn't know about anything at all in the world other than bicycle gears.

Wrabness *n.*
The feeling after having tried to dry oneself with a damp towel.

Writtle *vb.*
Of a steel ball, to settle into a hole.

Wroot *n.*
A short little berk who thinks that by pulling on his pipe and gazing shrewdly at you he will give the impression that he is infinitely wise and 6ft 2in.

Wubin *n.*
The metal foil container which Chinese meals come in.

Wyoming *ptcpl.vb.*
Moving in hurried desperation from one
cubicle to another in a public lavatory trying
to find one which has a lock on the door,
a seat on the bowl and no brown streaks on
the seat.

Y

Yalardy *n.*
An illness which you know you've got but which
the thermometer refuses to acknowledge.

Yarmouth *vb.*
To shout at foreigners in the belief that
the louder you speak, the better they'll
understand you.

Yate *n.*
Dishearteningly white piece of bread which
sits lumpily in a pop-up toaster during a
protracted throcking (q.v.) session.

Yebra *n.*
A cross between a zebra and anything else
which fancies zebras.

Yesnaby *n.*
A 'yes, maybe' which means 'no'.

Yetman *n.*
A yesman waiting to see who it would be most advantageous to agree with.

Yonder Bognie *n.*
The kind of restaurant advertised as 'just three minutes from this cinema' which clearly nobody ever goes to and, even if they had ever contemplated it, have certainly changed their minds since seeing the advert.

Yonkers *n.*
(RARE) The combined thrill of pain and shame when being caught in public plucking your nostril hairs and stuffing them into your side pocket.

York *vb.*
To shift the position of the shoulder straps on a heavy bag or rucksack in a vain attempt to make it seem lighter.

Hence: to laugh falsely and heartily at an unfunny remark.

'Jasmine yorked politely, loathing him to the depths of her being.' – Virginia Woolf.

Z

Zafrilla *n.*
A garment that even Grayson Perry would not deign to wear.

Zagreb *n.*
A stranger who suddenly clutches an intimate part of your body and then pretends they did it to prevent themselves falling.

Zeal Monachorum *n.*
(SKIING) To ski with zeal monachorum is to descend the top three-quarters of the mountain in a quivering blue funk, but on arriving at the gentle bit just in front of the restaurant to whizz to a stop like a victorious slalom champion.

Zeerust *n.*
The particular kind of datedness which afflicts things that were originally designed to look futuristic.

[184]

Zigong *n.*
Screeching skid made by cartoon character prior to turning round and running back in the opposite direction.

Zlatibor *n.*
(HUNGARIAN) A prince of the blood royal temporarily forced to seek employment as a waiter.

Zod *n.*
An irritating lump which sticks out from the main body. Hence:
(1) A bit of cement which sits proud of the brickwork.
(2) A drip of paint on the windowpane.
(3) The knob of surplus butter on a corner of toast.
(4) Noel Edmonds' head.

Zumbo *n.*
One who pretends not to know that the exhaust has fallen off his car.

INDEX OF MEANINGS

A

ABUSE
scissor: *Nogdam End*
self, post: *Sloinge*
self, sinister: *Southwick*

ACQUAINTANCES
remote: *Ardcrony*
who should be more remote:
Corfu

ACRONYMS, uselessness of: *Cafu*

ACTORS
dreadful, amateur: *Aberbeeg*
dreadful, fruity: *Hordle*
dreadful, lopsided: *Oundle*
dreadful, obese: *Pantperthog*
dreadful, Scottish, cravat-
wearing: *Glenduckie*
dreadful, Shakespearian:
Damnaglaur
dreadful, stained: *Multan*

AFTERNOON
four o'dock in the: *Brymbo*,
Farnham
wasted in front of the
television: *Gonnabarn*

AIRPORTS
behaviour of luggage in:
Adlestrop
cursed: *Aird of Sleat*

ALARMS
burglar: *Framlingham*
false: *Godalming*
silent: *Duleek*

untimely: *Lostwithiel*

ALBANIA, unpleasant beverages
of: *Naas*

ALGAE, trouser: *Huttoft*

AMERICANS
brain-dead: *Lackawanna*
strange, hairy: *Scethrog*
who aren't fooling anybody:
Ompton

AMOUNTS
contentious: *Bodmin*
footling: *Kibblesworth*
piddling: *Le Touquet*

ANATOMY
alarming discoveries about
someone's: *Wartnaby*
close proximity between bits
of: *Moisie*
confusion between bits of:
Willimantic
corrugations on bits of:
Plumgarths, *Des Moines*
horrible bits of: *Aigburth*
huge dangly strands of:
Ullingswick
hunts for bits of: *Tullynessle*
lovers who are keen on bits of
your: *Lublin*
odd connections between bits
of: *Acklins*
strangers who are keen on bits
of your: *Zagreb*
sweaty bits of: *Elsrickle*, *Pitsligo*
too frequently honoured parts
of: *Dubbo*

unwelcome bits of somebody
else's: *Stibb*
useless bits of: *Brecon, Clun*
wide open bits of: *Scugog*

ANIMALS
attempts to communicate with
Post Office clerks or: *Stoke Poges*
casual cross-breeding of: *Yebra*
digestive systems of: *Wendens
Ambo*
disgusting bits of: *Gruids*
disinclination to be bothered to
identify: *Parrog, Roosebeck*
doo-doos of (china): *Barstibley*
doo-doos of (metaphorical):
Euphrates, Old Cassop
doo-doos of (real): *Dogdyke,
Joliette, Bromsgrove*
eviscerated, Swedish: *Skannerup*
fried: *Toronto*
haughty: *Pofadder*
mythical, or at least
unrecognizable: *Polyphant*
things that are like bits of:
Scurlage
with absurd numbers of
stomachs: *Wendens Ambo*

ANKLES
bits above your: *Bogue*
corrugated: *Plumgarths*

ANORAKS
cosmopolitan: *Savernake*
nylon: *Screeb*

ANSWERS
deflected: *Ainderby Steeple*
expected: *Nome*
required, embarrassing: *Sneem*
the phone, confusion caused
when someone: *Gammersgill*
the phone, suspicion caused
when someone: *Kurdistan*
unwelcome, interminable:
Spurger

ANTIQUES
telephone: *Aldclune*

useless, definitely fake: *Brumby*
useless, possibly fake: *Lydd*

ANTS, means of chasing: *Monks
Toft*

APOLOGIES
loud, interminable: *Hickling*
recursive: *Greeley*
uttered while hopping: *Droitwich*

APPLAUSE
calculated to generate: *Firebag*
for injury: *Hoddlesdon*
ironic, in canteen: *Risplith*

ARCHDEACONS, protuberances
on the noses of: *Botolphs*

ARGUMENTS
after meals: *Bodmin*
after parties: *Heanton
Punchardon*
badly planned: *Eakring*
before meals: *Lowther*
chilly consequences of:
Famagusta
imperceptibly reversed:
Glenties
manifestly blithering:
Inverinate
uncharacteristically pertinent:
Gress

ARMHOLES
difficulties with: *Hessle*
excessive number of: *Jurby*

ARMRESTS, double helping of:
Rochester

ARMS
expanding: *Penge*
limp: *Oundle*
sweat under: *Pitsligo*

AROMAS
domestic, unwelcome: *Keele*
hireable, unwelcome: *Duluth*
rural, welcome: *Hull*
urban, unwelcome: *Chicago*
urban, welcome: *Lindisfarne*

ARTS
ancient, Eastern: *Kalami*

ancient: *Alltami*
domestic, sculptural: *Hepple*

ASHTRAYS
things used as: *Slumbay*
washing of: *Keele*

ASLEEP
bits of you that are: *Clun*
bits of you that aren't any
more: *Tingewick*
things collected while:
Ambatolampy
things heard while: *Balzan,
Bonkle*

ASSISTANTS
exorcists': *Clenchwarton*
plumbers': *Suckley Knowl*
shop: *Hotagen*

ATTACHMENT
to a face: *Kirby*
to a Hoover: *Swelling*
to a nose: *Botolphs*
to a string: *Scremby*

ATTACKS
spasmodic: *Jawcraig*
vampire: *Spittal of Glenshee*

ATTEMPTS
kindly, misguided: *Kirby
Misperton*
lecherous, resolute: *Tullynessle*
lecherous, unsuccessful:
Farrancassidy
to see the film you've paid good
money to watch: *Ossining*

AWNINGS, gushing: *Sotterley*

B

BABIES
muckiness of: *Papple*
stickiness of: *Halcro*
second thoughts about the
names of: *Abert*

BACKS
of armchairs: *Hassop*

of cupboards: *Cong*
of people who are not your
friends: *Boothby Graffoe*
of T-shirts: *Wedderlairs*
of taxis: *Low Ardwello*
of throats: *Gulberwick*
things dropped down: *Burton
Coggles*

BACKSLAPPING: *Boothby Graffoe*
BADER, SIR DOUGLAS: *Ludlow*
BAFFLEMENT, nuptials marked
by: *Cowcaddens*

BAGS
carrier, growing: *Dungeness*
elderly, deaf: *Nanhoron*
fearsome, hideous: *Baughurst*
mulch kept in the bottom of:
Glud
plastic, maternal: *Marlow*
slippery, translucent: *Flimby*
solitary, Scottish: *Glentaggart*

BAKERS
least appealing products of:
Brymbo
people who show off to:
Bradworthy

BALDNESS
graceless reactions to:
Ugglebarnby
useless attempts to conceal:
Scraptoft

BALLADS, raucous old: *Banteer*
BALLS
dangerous number of: *Belding*
soggy, hairy: *Polperro*
steel, rattling: *Writtle*

BANDS, rubber: *Monks Toft*
BANKS
rising young managers of:
Hobarris
things that confuse:
Albuquerque, Screggan
Welsh: *Pentre-tafarn-y-fedw*

BARMEN
aimless: *Todding*

apparently blind: *Epping*
surly: *Goole*

BARRISTERS
dancing: *Stelling Minnis*
greasy: *Glazeley*

BARS
complete berks in: *Louth*
sandwich: *Darenth*
theatre: *Tabley Superior*
wet: *Listowel, Goole*

BASINS
things found in: *Misool, Hathersage*
things washed in: *Paradip*

BASTARDS
bloody rude: *Fovant*
in technical sense: *Gastard*
inconsiderate, stupid, filthy: *Dogdyke*
lazy: *Abinger, Ozark*
mad and/or lazy: *Boseman*
scatty: *Abligo*
six year old: *Little Urswick*
smooth, beery; *Louth*
smooth, young: *Shirmers*
smug, Masonic: *Grimsby*
vile, vain, rich: *Shalunt*

BATHROOMS
attempts to lure people out of: *Visby*
nocturnal attempts to find: *Islesteps*

BATHS
bubbly noises in: *Budle*
prunelike objects in: *Dewlish*
round, rubbery objects in: *Dillytop*
soggy things in: *Polperro*
turbulent convection in: *Harlosh*

BATS
hairy, harmless old: *Lossiemouth*
incompetent, well-meaning old: *Jurby*
stout, wooden: *Pelutho*

vampire: *Spittal of Glenshee*

BATTLEAXES, sharp, on castle wall: *Pabbay*

BDDBBRRDDBDDRR, things that go: *Thrupp*

BEATING: *Aboyne*

BED
areas to be avoided in: *Hobbs Cross*
banana-shaped objects on: *Baumber*
comforting preparations for: *Lambarene*
dreadful mistakes in: *Hagnaby*
tent-shaped objects in: *Visby*
things found in: *Ballycumber*
things that bounce on: *Abwong, Dunster*
things that don't work in: *Stutton*
things that go wrong in: *Brecon*
things that jump out of: *Duleek*
thrashing around in: *Oswestry*
unwelcome lumps in: *Tolob*

BEDROOMS
chilly winds in: *Famagusta*
embarrassing things in hotel: *Bedfont*
emerging from wrong: *Sheepy Magna*
guests in spare: *Dunster*
views into other people's: *Beaulieu Hill*
young girls': *Tibshelf*

BEHAVIOUR
facetious, misguided: *Dockery*
lip: *Gallipoli*
naughty: *Sheepy Magna*
nerdlike: *Scugog*
perverse, sticky: *Ardslignish*

BEHIND
cleavage in: *Ravenna*
dragging one leg: *Oundle*
droplets on: *Elsrickle*
leaving one's hat: *Hidcote Bartram*

[190]

BELGIANS, hairy, religious: *Scethrog*

BELIEFS
creamy, mistaken: *Teignmouth*
fatuous, entertained abroad: *Valletta, Yarmouth*
mistaken, humorous: *Dockery*

BERKS
check-jacketed, beery: *Louth*
deliberately forgetful: *Abligo*
in restaurants: *Ardentinny*
irritatingly conversational: *Dalmilling*
lazy: *Nybster*
short, pipe-smoking: *Wroot*
unwanted: *Nubbock*
who can't tell jokes without making a complete hash of it: *Jofane*

BICYCLE GEARS: *Wormelow Tump*

BILLS
anomalous: *Bodmin*
heart-stopping: *Squibnocket*
sneakily inflated: *Winston-Salem*

BIRD
Brazilian, easily amused: *Waccamaw*
possible congruence with type of: *Parrog*
sort of half-: *Polyphant*
unidentifiable: *Roosebeck*

BIROS
holes in: *Pluvigner*
leaky: *Pentre-tafarn-y-fedw*
three-coloured: *Ospringe*
tied together, six: *Ipplepen*

BISCUITS
digestive, religious: *Corstorphine*
fresh, or so they claim: *Dorridge*

BITES
snakes which can't be bothered to administer: *Pofadder*
spots which could be: *Bauple*

BLISS
conjugal, absence of at dinner: *Balemartine, Inigonish*
conjugal, absence of in bed: *Famagusta*
conjugal, absence of in car: *Heanton Punchardon*
conjugal, conducted on cheap floor-matting: *Bures*
conjugal, first steps back towards: *Manitoba*
conjugal, invitation to: *Visby*
conjugal, possible threats to: *Kurdistan*
conjugal, recurrent threats to: *Mavis Enderby*
of a really good widdle: *Gilling*

BLOBS
bloody-minded: *Glossop*
dried: *Klosters*
stubborn: *Quenby*

BLOWOUTS, oral: *Berkhamsted*

BLUE FUNK: *Zeal Monachorum*

BLUE MURDER: *Timble*

BOARDS, don't forget: *Scremby*

BOOK REVIEWS: *Ripon*

BOOKS
codswallop in: *Pulverbatch*
fat, expensive: *Great Tosson*
futile attempts to read: *Dalmilling*
incomprehensible paragraphs in: *Fritham*
lavatorial: *Great Wakering*
of matches, not worth stealing: *Fremantle*
triumphantly finished: *Beppu*
you haven't finished: *Ballycumber*
you haven't read at all: *Bathel*

BOOKSHELVES: *Ahenny*

BORES
low tolerance of: *Lolland*
pompous, any age: *Ardcrony*
principal habitat of: *Burslem*

things induced by: *Wawne*
worst, at a party: *West Wittering*
BOTTLE PARTIES: *Naas, Aasleagh*
BOTTLES
blue: *Bursledon*
gin: *Le Touquet*
ketchup: *Cromarty*
whisky: *Brumby*
BOTTOM
chill wind that afflicts: *Famagusta*
cleavage in workman's: *Ravenna*
exposed: *Grinstead*
huge whirling brushes on: *Vancouver*
interesting patterns on own: *Kettering*
lip: *Gallipoli*
newly cleaned: *Riber*
of drawers, things found in: *Pimlico*
of shoes: *Luppitt*
reaction of Brazilian bird to mention of: *Waccamaw*
rivulets between cheeks of: *Elsrickle*
warmth of someone else's: *Shoeburyness*
BOXES
of chocolates: *Bolsover*
in garages: *Kentucky*
BOYLE, FRANKIE: *Maaruig*
BOYS
high-pitched: *Caarnduncan*
new: *Percyhorner*
with stupid names: *Cheb*
BRAIN
inoperative: *Duntish*
of coffee machine: *Uttoxeter*
BRAS
impossible: *Farrancassidy*
inadequate: *Lusby*
BREAD
airborne crumbs of: *Satterthwaite*
hundred slices of: *Darenth*

single slice of: *Yate*
wildlife in: *Mankinholes*
BREAK
a leg: *Thurnby*
into something that clearly isn't a run: *Sturry*
something you've just glued together: *Soller*
the ice: *Wivenhoe*
up, are they going to?: *Badachonacher*
BREASTS
attempted access to: *Farrancassidy*
clumsy business with: *Meadle*
lopsided: *Preston Gubbals*
only semi-contained: *Lusby*
BREATH
condensation of: *Brithdir*
extruded through noses: *Burbage*
BREEZES, in armpit: *Kimmeridge*
BRISTLES: *Aith*
BRUISES
honourably acquired: *Dubbo*
virulent, accidental: *Sluggan*
yellowing, inexplicable: *Ampus*
BUBBLES
behind wallpaper: *Lupridge*
congealed, cheesy: *Eriboll*
flatulent: *Budle*
slurped, milky: *Pitlochry*
BUFFERS
boring, old: *Ainderby Quernhow*
insane, sprightly old: *Wivenhoe*
loathsome, merry old: *Boothby Graffoe*
pompous old: *Ainderby Steeple*
BUILDERS
bottoms of: *Ravenna*
murderous: *Hodnet*
rubble-removing techniques of: *Shottle*
BULBS
light: *Fring*

that die when you look at them: *Lutton Gowts*

Bulges
cheesy: *Eriboll*
huge, erotic: *Humby*
medium-sized, erotic: *Huby*
persistent, unwanted: *Lower Peover*
prestressed: *Bromsgrove*
pustular: *Bilbster*
tiny, erotic: *Budby*
unwelcome, obvious: *Stebbing*

Bumps
in slimming biscuits: *Naples*
on plastic trays: *Bolsover*

Bunches, useless: *Burton Coggles*

Buns: *Brymbo*

Burglars: *Taroom*

Burns, non-poetic: *Hutlerburn*

Buses
coats on: *Moffat*
desires aroused by: *Abercrave*
Italian, overdue: *Stagno di Gumbi*
oversized: *Articlave*
parts of: *Edgbaston*

Buttons
bacony: *Beccles*
conversations which feature views on: *Gussage*
tummy: *Lowestoft*

C

Cabers, misthrown: *Comer*

Cafés, nasty: *Cromarty*

Cameras, wrong: *Hosmer*

Candles, deformed: *Slubbery*

Cans
aerosol, rattly: *Millinocket*
tin: *Boscastle*

Cardboard
boxes, satisfying: *Kentucky*
insane amount of: *Dorridge*

prematurely discarded: *Nottage*
wedges of folded: *Ludlow*

Cards
identity, loss of: *Margate*
leaving, insincerity of: *Berriwillock*
that have to be removed: *Rickling*

Carol singers, avoidance of: *Fulking*

Car parks, automatic: *Nad*

Carpets
rucked up edges of: *Thurnby*
things found on: *Silloth*
things littered on: *Blitterlees*

Cars
appalling expense of repairing: *Squibnocket*
appallingly noisy: *Zumbo*
berks in: *Noak Hoak*
chasing each other: *Imber*
fat chance of getting anywhere useful in: *Brindle*
fat chance of getting into: *Delfibble*
fat chance of getting your coat clean again after being in: *Fladderbister*
in huddle on motorways: *Grimbister*
invisible bits of: *Stibbard*
parked, hooting at: *Tooting Bec*
steering wheels of: *Tarabulus*
things found under seats of: *Belper*
travelling, producing gibberish: *Addis Ababa*
unhuddled on motorways: *Jalingo*
unsecured contents of: *Scackleton*

Cartoons
cheaply produced effects in: *Drumsna*
conveniently situated pieces of vegetation in: *Grimmet*

expressions on faces of
characters in: *Ghent*
sparing use of: *Great Tosson*
sudden turns effected in:
Zigong
CASSEROLE
elk-liver, Swedish: *Skannerup*
week-old, dried: *Pott Shrigley*
CAVITIES
definitely unhygienic: *Glutt
Lodge, Henstridge*
probably unhygienic:
Mankinholes
CEILINGS
elderly decorations still on:
Chenies
geniuses not getting on with:
Stagno di Gumbi
CELEBRITIES
camp: *Melbury Bubb*
conspicuous: *Sloothby*
CHAIRS
dismantled: *Blitterlees*
marks left by wickerwork:
Kettering
plastic, sweaty: *Skibbereen*
plastic, wheezing: *Essendine*
CHAMBERMAIDS, grisly
discoveries of: *Bedford*
CHANGE
bacon-saving: *Nupend*
name: *Aalst, Abert*
naughty business with:
Bindle
of mind about where to eat:
Yonder Bognie
pitch at the last moment:
Detchant
small: *Boolteens*
wet: *Goole*
CHARM
infuriatingly over-endowed
with: *Offord Darcy, Draffan*
lack of: *Winter*
resistant to: *Udine*

woolly, distant: *Sheppey*
CHEEK
astonishment at one's own:
Coodardy
movements of: *Humber*
noise made by: *Garvock*
noise made while kissing:
Kabwum
CHEERFUL
about to become a bit more:
Mointy
manner of arising from bed:
Spreakley
manner of bouncing on bed:
Abwong
manner of going to Cornwall:
Offleyhoo
CHEESE
burnt bubble of: *Eriboll*
cottage: *Berkhamsted*
grater, unwashed: *Abinger*
various sizes of: *Fraddam*
CHEFS, loud wallies who call for:
Haugham
CHESS: *Bishop's Caundle*
CHEWING GUM: *Belper*
CHILDREN
small, bouncing: *Dunster*
small, insistent: *Nazeing*
small, in glasses: *Goginan*
small, inconvenient: *Glassel*
small, reminiscent of Jackson
Pollock: *Polyphant, Smearisary*
small, rude, innocent: *Sneem*
small, sticky: *Badgebup*
small, untalented: *Papcastle*
small, with long legs: *Abruzzo*
small, yelling: *Timble*
CHOCOLATES: *Bolsover, Cannock
Chase*
CHUCKLES, chummy: *Lybster*
CHUMMINESS, man-to-man:
Tillicoultry
CIGARETTES
in lager, ends of: *Slumbay*

meaningless rituals involving: *Pocking*

problems of smoking untipped: *Scopwick*

unfairly acquired: *Winston-Salem*

CINEMA

just three minutes from this: *Yonder Bognie*

people who've just been to the: *Lowther*

seats, monopolization of: *Rochester*

swaying about in: *Imber, Ossining*

CLEANING LADIES

conversations to avoid having with: *Clabby*

pre-empting: *Spofforth*

CLEANING, DRY: *Knaptoft*

CLEAVAGES

in bottoms: *Ravenna*

speleological, monstrous: *Simprim*

CLEVER

architecturally: *Articlave*

but lazy: *Ible*

decreasingly: *Mogumber*

tactics, useless: *Aboyne*

CLIFFTOPS

silly little kids on: *Caarnduncan*

noise issuing from: *Craboon*

CLINGFILM: *Amlwch*

CLIPPERS

gaff-rigged: *Kanturk*

ticket collectors': *Didcot*

CLOCKS

alarm, faulty: *Duleek*

alarm, unnecessary: *Dunster*

Cuckoo: *Penge*

CLOTS, mad, patronizing: *Largoward*

CODGERS

boring, famous, old: *Boothby Graffoe*

huge, wobbling, wheezing, old: *Kingston Bagpuise*

stuffy, medieval, old: *Warleggan*

COFFEE

not quite enough: *Pidney*

noxious substances in: *Cadomin*

COFFEE MACHINES, intelligent: *Uttoxeter*

COINS

domestic, vital: *Nupend*

foreign, assorted: *Boolteens*

foreign, unwanted: *Bindle*

COLD

ears, hearty feelings induced by: *Luffness*

swimming pool, nearly brave enough to dive into: *Parbold*

third recurrence of winter: *Snoul*

taps, hot and deft handling of: *Alltami*

COLLECTIONS

awful record: *Hextable*

charity: *Ardelve*

eccentric: *Aldclune*

somnambulent: *Ambatolampy*

COLOUR

biros, three-: *Ospringe*

depressingly wrong: *Gretna Green*

multi-purpose, municipal: *Frating Green*

of paints in catalogues: *Wasp Green*

red, virulent: *Buldoo*

supplements, hideous containers for: *Mapledurham*

COMBS, clogged: *Haselbury Plucknett*

COMPLAINTS

tiresome: *Mogumber*

very tiresome: *Ainderby Quernhow*

COMPONENTS

small, meaningless: *Pimlico*

vital, missing: *Exeter*

CONCEPTS
  hitherto unnamed: *Liff*
  that people won't grasp
  perfectly simple: *Osbaston*
CONFETTI
  overabundance of: *Pathstruie*
  royal: *Didcot*
CONTAINERS
  Chinese meal: *Wubin*
  ludicrously misnamed: *Sadberge*
CONTEST, bagpipe: *Spittal of Glenshee*
CONTRIBUTIONS
  negligible: *Spoffard*
  very public, probably
  negligible: *Ardelve*
CONVERSATIONS
  desired: *Affcot*
  gaps in: *Samalaman*
  interminable: *Ditherington*
  polite, interminable: *Clabby*
  polite, pointless: *Sittingbourne*
  shifting: *Glenties*
  thuggish: *Jawf*
  wasted: *Harpenden*
CORDS
  electrical, that get pulled back:
  Lynwilg
  swimming-trunk, that get lost:
  Lubcroy
CORNWALL, mood on
  contemplating trip to: *Offleyhoo*
CORRIDORS
  cowardly behaviour in:
  Corriecravie
  etiquette in: *Corriearklet*
  hideous mistimings in:
  Corriemoillie
  making pig's ear of walking
  down: *Corriemuchloch*
  pretending to be Richard Briers
  in: *Corriedoo, Corrievorrie*
COSIES
  spare toilet-roll: *Ossett*
  tea: *Kitmurvy*

COTTAGES
  retirement: *Duncraggon*
  weekend: *Hull*
COUGHS
  gurgling: *Brisbane*
  that don't seem to have any
  effect: *Gulberwick*
  throaty: *Dorchester*
COUPLES
  arguing loudly: *Heanton Punchardon*
  arguing most of the time:
  Badachonacher
  arguing silently: *Famagusta*
  no longer arguing: *Manitoba*
  pretending not to be arguing:
  Nyarling
COWS
  journeys through: *Wendens Ambo*
  things left in fields by:
  Munderfield
CRAFTWORK: *Dalrymple*
CRAVAT, worn by Scottish actors:
  Glenduckie
CREAM
  anti-wrinkle: *Melton Constable*
  ice: *Badgebup*
CREEPS
  boring: *West Wittering*
  embarrassing realization about
  identity of: *East Wittering*
CRIMES, ancient: *Burlingjobb*
CRISES, humorous exploitation
  of: *Gribun*
CROSS
  a road too slowly: *Sturry*
  a road, not about to: *Boseman*
  activities indulged in while:
  Burleston
  things that make you: *Draffan, Hickling*
  with zebra: *Yebra*
CROSSINGS
  pedestrian: *Boseman*
  train: *Trantlemore*

[196]

CROTCHES, trouser: *Botley,*
Piddletrenthide
CROUCHES, upward: *Hucknall*
CRY
end of a: *Mointy*
ill-equipped to: *Hankate*
reason to: *Babworth*
CUBICLES
inaccessible: *Milwaukee*
horribly soiled: *Wyoming*
CUPBOARDS
bathroom, attempts to lure
people out of: *Visby*
jugs in: *Upottery*
kites in: *Kanturk*
saucepans in: *Cong*
skeletons in: *Glemanuilt*
CURSES, Scottish: *Aird of Sleat*
CUSHIONS, roadside: *Edgbaston*

D

DAMOCLES, the Trewoofe of:
Trewoofe
DANCES
in street: *Droitwich, Stelling*
Minnis
of beer glasses: *Sketty*
people who won't ask people
for: *Peening Quarter*
Polynesian, that the Queen has
to sit through: *Grutness*
DEARIES
lovable, mad, old: *Bradworthy*
soporific, rabbity, old: *Clabby*
DECISIONS
minor, agonizing: *Deventer*
right, agonizing: *Abalemma*
wrong, agonizing: *Huna*
DECORATIONS, CHRISTMAS:
Clovis, Chenies
DENTISTS
activities of unemployed:
Beccles

results of going to: *Gallipoli,*
Gipping
DEPARTURES
inability to make: *Foffarty*
of madmen: *Throckmorton*
welcome, of others: *Nubbock*
DEPOSITS
crystalline: *Libenge, Klosters*
pink, sticky: *Glud*
sludgy: *Cromarty*
small, black, satisfying: *Tidpit*
DESKS
useful things that fall off: *Tampa*
useless things that stay on:
Kilvaxter
DESPERATION
polite: *Iping*
frankly rushed: *Wyoming*
DETERMINATION
bloody-minded: *Oswestry*
politely restrained: *Kent,*
Calicut, Smarden
DEVICES
agricultural: *Jarrow*
humorous: *Barstibley*
immensely complex: *Uttoxeter*
DIALOGUE, single page of:
Clackavoid
DIARIES, meaningless entries
in: *Epsom*
DIARRHOEA, verbal: *Ainderby*
Steeple, Spurger
DICE: *Hoggeston*
DIRECTION
almost certainly the wrong:
Brindle
opposite: *Zigong, Droitwich*
without any apparent:
Chimkent
DIRECTIONS: difficulties of
remembering: *Dinder*
DIRT
on overalls of fraudulent
workmen: *Podebrady*
types of: *Sutton and Cheam*

DISCO
    people who should have been
    left in the: *Hagnaby*
    people who skulk in corners of
    the: *Peening Quarter*

DISCREPANCIES, unaccountable:
    Bodmin

DISEASES
    conveniently debilitating:
    Patkai Bum
    of plants, artificial: *Breckles*
    of plants, likely to be induced:
    Lutton Gowts
    unrecognized by medical
    science: *Yalardy, Leazes*

DISHWASHERS: *Dobwalls*

DOG-OWNERS, cretinous:
    Dogdyke

DOGS
    large, randy, teatime: *Scrabster*
    neat deposits made by French:
    Joliette
    small, moribund: *Scamblesby*
    small, repulsive, snuffling:
    Scorrier
    small, vicious, yappy: *Baughurst*

DOORS
    carelessly closed car:
    Fladderbister
    deliberately obstructive:
    Ramsgate
    elevator: *Emsworth*
    lockless: *Wyoming, Milwaukee*
    revolving, overpopulated:
    Shifnal
    things caused by walking into:
    Sluggan
    things precariously balanced
    above: *Trewoofe*

DOORSTEP, people you don't
    want to see on your: *Corfu*

DOUBLE GLAZING, inhabitants
    of: *Harbottle*

DRAWBRIDGES, mischievously
    raised: *Araglin*

DRAWERS
    bottom: *Marlow*
    things found in: *Pimlico,*
    Burton Coggles

DRESSING TABLES
    small coins found on: *Boolteens*
    things found on hotel: *Lamlash*

DRIBBLE
    infantile: *Halcro*
    somnolent: *Sompting*
    waxy: *Slubbery*

DRINK
    feigned reluctance to: *Alcoy*
    nipping off for a quick:
    Lochranza
    philosophical state during:
    Solent

DRINKS
    effects of respectable: *Richmond*
    repellent: *Aasleagh, Naas*
    small, long-lasting: *Stody*
    spilt: *Tulsa*

DRIPS
    gooey, waxen: *Slubbery*
    paint: *Zod*

DROPLETS
    hanging, stylish: *Berry Pomeroy*
    hanging, mobile: *Longniddry*
    persistent, trouser: *Wimbledon*

DRUNKS
    methods of detecting:
    Tolstachaolais
    peckish: *Pott Shrigley*
    unappealing: *Pleeley*
    uncomprehending: *Blithbury*

DRY, not very: *Wrabness*

DUFFERS, barking-mad old:
    Pant-y-Wacco

DUSTBINS
    early warning: *Tananarive*
    nasty bits at the bottom of: *Eads*
    nocturnal behaviour of lids of:
    Balzan
    uses for plastic: *Shottle*

DWARFS, nubile: *Forsinain*

E

EARS
fears concerning: *Loberia*
inner: *Nanhoron, Ulting*
outer: *Luffness*

EARTHQUAKES, humorous:
Drumsna

EDICTS, ancient: *Farduckmanton*

EGGS
boiled: *Symonds Yat*
coffee drunk from receptacle
designed for: *Snover*
scrambled: *Cloates Point*

EIGHTY-YEAR-OLDS, bounding,
refrigerated: *Wivenhoe*

ELBOWS
damp: *Listowel*
sexually active, sore: *Bures*
territorially intrusive:
Rochester

EMOTIONS
angry, unmusical: *Burleston*
cheerful: *Spreakley, Abwong*
infinitely sad: *Glasgow*
susceptibility of: *Cahors*
triste: *Sloinge*

ENDS
damp, cigarette: *Slumbay*
long, thin, dangling: *Ranfurly*
of desks, uses of: *Thrupp*
of parties: *Aasleagh*
of recalcitrant pieces of cotton:
Vidlin
of toothbrushes: *Pibsbury*

ENGINEERS, telephone,
inexplicable marriages to:
Lydiard Tregoze

ENTRIES
in diaries: *Epsom*
in drive: *Tananarive*
into Mecca: *Multan*
into the Kingdom of Heaven:
Vidlin

ENVELOPES
dangerous: *Scramoge*
deceitful: *Hugglescote*
empty: *Cannock Chase*

ENVIRONMENTS
dark, moist: *Huttoft*
urban, excremental: *Bromsgrove*

EPAULETTES, useless: *Trossachs*

EPIGLOTTIS, giant, waggling:
Ullingswick

ERASERS, rubber: *Tampa*

ESKIMO, sore thumbs of an:
Anantnag

EVENINGS
Friday, noisy: *Framlingham*
tense: *Heanton Punchardon*
wasted: *Lowther*

EVENTS, lack of: *Chimkent*

EX-GIRLFRIEND
new boyfriend of: *Rudge*
wife's resentment of: *Mavis
Enderby*

EXCRETA, airborne: *Burlingjobb*

EXCUSES
feeble: *Dorridge*
impromptu, but still feeble:
Hastings
incredible, unnecessary:
Falster
indignant: *Hoff*
ludicrous: *Brisbane*
transparent: *Bilbster*

EXORCISM: *Clenchwarton*

EXPERIENCES
hitherto unnamed: *Liff*
horrific: *Maaruig*
lurching: *Bedfont*
melancholy: *Glasgow*
panicky: *Ditherington*
satisfying: *Skellow*
terrific: *Nempnett Thrubwell*

EXPERTS, humiliating the:
Aboyne

EXPRESS, THE SUNDAY, people
who actually read the: *Molesby*

EXPRESSIONS
facial, agonized:
Minchinhampton
peculiar: *Banff*
pissed: *Blithbury*
raging: *Damnaglaur*
sly: *Golant*
vaguely attentive: *Hove*

EYEBROWS
things that grow between: *Tew*
useless employment of: *Epping*

F

FACES
grubby: *Badgebup*
guilty: *Peru*, *Hastings*
silly: *Leeming*, *Banff*
warm and salty: *Moisie*

FAMILY
arguments, odd behaviour
during: *Gress*
fictional, head of: *Potarch*
hats that don't belong to the:
Tweedsmuir
Royal, head of the, being stoic
in Indonesia: *Grutness*
Royal, joke-telling privileges
of the: *Princes Risborough*
Royal, member of foreign, on
uppers: *Zlatibor*
Royal, sleeping with members
of the: *Randers*
Royal, understandable fears
suffered by members of the:
Loberia
seaside-visiting: *Molesby*

FARTS – *see under noises* (if you
must)

FAT
books: *Great Tosson*
chance of actually winning
£10,000: *Hugglescote*
ends of ties: *Ranfurly*

people: *Humber*
solicitors: *Valletta*

FEARS
anatomical: *Loberia*
vegetable: *Peoria*

FEELINGS
in unexpected parts of body:
Acklins
of fillings: *Tingrith*
of something or other,
profound: *Hambledon*
queasy, bottom-orientated:
Shoeburyness
queasy: *Guernsey*
sentimental: *Glasgow*
sofa-threatening: *Pollatomish*
tired, cold, thirsty: *Luffenham*
uneasy: *Dungeness*, *Frating
Green*

FEET
damp, pink, wrinkled: *Dewlish*
elephantine, umbrellas for the
use of: *Clackmannan*
painful: *Nipishish*
tingling sensations in: *Gilling*
with highly developed tap
skills: *Polbathic*

FENCING: *Pabbay*

FESTOONMENT: *Chipping Ongar*

FIFTEEN YEARS
at the same desk: *Brough
Sowerby*
younger than you, people who
are: *Glasgow*

FILMS
pornographic: *Papworth Everard*
rewritten ends of famous:
Epworth
that won't get made: *Spiddle*

FINGERS
definitely not green: *Lutton
Gowts*
insertion of, into: *Cannock Chase*
lecherous: *Farrancassidy*,
Tullynessle

[200]

not within reach of: *Nad*
things that cling to:
Mummelgum, Ardslignish,
Dipple
FISH
tropical, stupid: *Stoke Poges*
overabundance of heads of:
Chimbote
FLAMES
almost-completely-forgotten
old: *Mavis Enderby*
people you wish were old:
Lydiard Tregoze
reminders of old: *Mavesyn*
Ridware
FLAPS
clothy, roomy: *Moffat*
hairy, sparse: *Scraptoft*
leathery: *Luppitt*
muddy: *Fladderbister*
FLATS
grimy: *Torlundy*
too far from the shops:
Nantwich
FLEMING, SIR ALEXANDER:
Eriboll
FLIES: *Harbottle*
FLOOR-MATTING, indelicate uses
of: *Bures*
FLUFF
mysterious: *Knaptoft*
navel: *Lowestoft*
yellow: *Memphis*
FOLDS
bothersome: *Tolob*
fleshy: *Lusby*
silky: *Shrenk*
FOOD
ethnic, inedible: *Chimbote*
inappropriate: *Kowloon*
misnamed: *Slabberts*
railway, inedible: *Amlwch*
sculptable: *Hepple*
shortly going to be inedible:
Cloates Point

unequal divisions of: *Finuge*
very little actual, packets
containing: *Dorridge*
FOOTBALLERS, pansy:
Hoddlesdon
FOREIGNERS
impersonation of: *Aberbeeg*
probably deaf or stupid:
Yarmouth
FOREPLAY
at a distance: *Visby*
clumsy: *Meadle*
reconciliatory: *Manitoba*
vocal: *Low Ardwello*
FOWL-FEEDING: *Farduckmanton*
FREEMASONS
banned practices of: *Enumclaw*
ritual pieces of gristle, use of
by: *Grimsby*
FRIDGES
concealed matter in: *Goosnargh*
concealed matter rediscovered
three weeks later in: *High Offley*
damp things in: *Nantwich*
strips of floor next to: *Torlundy*
teeming with life: *Guernsey*
FRIENDS
or so they would like to think:
Peterculter, Ardcrony, Boothby
Graffoe
unmarried: *Canudos*
FROWNING, important:
Frolesworth
FRUIT
in the manner of: *Hordle*
stupid overabundance of:
Limassol
theft of a single piece of:
Market Deeping
FURNITURE
air-expelling: *Essendine*
bamboo, disintegration of:
Blitterlees
execrable: *Mapledurham*
lavatorial: *Ossett*

G

Gable, Clark: *Epworth*

Games
  ball: *Hoddlesdon, Pelutho*
  board: *Bishop's Caundle,*
    Hoggeston
  indoor: *Aboyne*
  outdoor, Eastern European:
    Twomileborris

Gardening
  equipment, piece of,
    mysterious: *Haxby*
  hopelessness of: *Crail*
  trousers used for: *Broats*

Gardens
  alarming sheds in: *Low*
    Eggborough
  embarrassing talks in: *Ambleside*

Garments
  discussions about making:
    Gussage
  ethnic, inapposite: *Nokomis*
  exotic, pretentious: *Shalunt*
  fatuous, foreign: *Valletta*
  funny one that man's wearing:
    Roosebeck
  gaberdine, ankle-length:
    Flodigarry
  loose, hateful, well-
    intentioned: *Anjozorobe*
  naff material for making: *Joplin*
  peculiar, frightful: *Neen Sollars*
  preposterous: *Zafrilla*
  removed with dispiriting
    results: *Wartnaby*
  semi-inverted: *Hessle*
  that don't fool anybody:
    Ompton
  too loose: *Shrenk*
  woollen, knee-length: *Jurby*

Gazes, shrewd, berkish: *Wroot*

Genitals
  moist: *Wetwang*

  moved about by owner: *Grobister*
  moved about by selves:
    Tingewick
  solitary recreational uses of:
    Southwick, Sloinge
  washed politely: *Paradip*
  well-groomed: *Spruce Knob*

Gestures, ambiguous but
  bloody rude: *Fovant*

Gibberish
  argumentative: *Inverinate*
  nocturnal: *Burslem*
  telephonic: *Harpenden,*
    Gammersgill
  that issues from cars: *Addis*
    Ababa

Gin, price of: *Le Touquet*

Girlfriend
  long forgotten except by wife:
    Mavis Enderby
  resentment concerning: *Rudge*

Girls
  coiffured: *Aubusson*
  naff epistolary habits of: *Ocilla*
  pot-brandishing: *Kittybrewster*
  teenage, in bedroom: *Tibshelf*

Gizmos
  plastic, metal, Bakelite: *Pimlico*
  small, clever: *Uttoxeter*
  tasteless: *Barstibley*

Glances
  humorous, at blobs: *Swanage*
  meaningful: *Balemartine*

Glass
  pointless scraping at: *Quenby*
  pointless tapping on: *Stoke*
    Poges

Globules, yellow, gummy,
  unpleasant: *Mugeary*

Go
  bbddbbddbbrrbrrrddrr, things
    that: *Thrupp*
  off, alarms that don't: *Duleek*
  people who finally: *Nubbock*
  people who just won't: *Clunes*

to the lavatory, urgent need to:
Great Wakering
trying unsuccessfully to: *Foffarty*

GOATS
jocular tedious old: *Barstibley*
noisy tuneless old: *Royston*

GOLFING, overpaid twats who go:
Kitmurvy

GOLF STROKES, homicidal:
Whaplode Drove

GOO
seagull: *Sutton and Cheam*
waxy: *Slubbery*

GOODBYES, premature: *Hidcote Bartram*

GOSSIP
bubbling with: *Malaybalay*
judicious applications of:
Marytavy
subject of immense amount of:
Tukituki

GOURMETS, slithery: *Berry Pomeroy*

GRASS
absence of: *Abruzzo*
intelligent forms of: *Trispen*

GRAVEL
infuriating: *Crail*
walking barefoot on: *Nipishish*

GREER, GERMAINE: *Shrivenham*

GRIDS, cattle: *Humber*

GROCERS, green: *Halifax, Smisby*

GROUND
things buried four feet in the:
Pymble
toxic waste: *Caarnduncan*
up: *Sadberge*
worn away: *Abruzzo*

GROUPS
infuriatingly indecisive: *Lowther*
of five that should be four:
Lampeter
peer: *Caarnduncan*
that exclude you: *Margaretting Tye*

GUARDS, railway: *Galashiels*

GUILT
powerful: *Glemanuilt*
surprised: *Peru*

GUMBOOTS
cold: *Luffness*
wet: *Burwash*

GUNGE
crystalline: *Libenge*
damp, gummy: *Deal*
green, shrubby: *Sadberge*
pinkish: *Glud*
unwholesome: *Mummelgum*

GURGLING
involuntary, abdominal: *Tumby*
perfectly reasonable
explanation for: *Brisbane*
through straws: *Pitlochry*

GUSTO, terrific, tuneless: *Royston*

GUTTERS, dog's business
clogging up the: *Dogdyke*

H

HAIR
armpit, ruffled: *Kimmeridge*
facial, bizarre: *Scethrog*
few last strands of: *Scraptoft*
greasy, legal: *Glazeley*
paint damage caused by: *Garrow*
plucking of nostril: *Yonkers*
pubic, in moussaka: *Scroggs*
sprigs of, for chasing ants:
Monks Toft
tufty interocular bits of: *Tew*
unaccompanied: *Albacete*
unbecoming styles of: *Aubusson, Ugglebarnby, Papigochic*

HANDLEBAR MOUSTACHES,
female: *Lossiemouth*

HANDS
clammy: *Meath*
psychologically helpful
movements of the: *Scosthrop*

rubbed: *Ardentinny*
slimy: *Scurlage*
HANGOVERS, incapacitating:
Duntish
HANKIES
lack of: *Hankate*
peered into: *Massachusetts*
worn on head: *Sidcup*
HAT behind, leaving one's:
Hidcote Bartram
HATRED, violent, by spouse:
Mavis Enderby
HATS
furry, absurd: *Glinsk*
gigantic, conical: *Valletta*
large, ill-fitting collection of:
Tweedsmuir
naff: *Sidcup*
HEADS
alarming numbers of fish:
Chimbote
black: *Quabbs*
of state, poorly: *Patkai Bum*
HEALTHY, hopeless attempts to
become: *Berkhamsted, Elgin,
Kingston Bagpuise*
HEDGE, things to do behind one's
front: *Todber*
HERRING FISHERMEN:
Flodigarry
HISTORY, lost in the mists of:
Hutlerburn
HOLES
bath overflow: *Polperro*
in biros: *Pluvigner*
in toothbrushes: *Pibsbury*
nefarious use of: *Pode Hole*
things which get stuck over:
Spuzzum
things which settle into: *Writtle*
things which sit on: *Dillytop*
HOLIDAYS
impressively unencumbered:
Nuncargate
naïve behaviour on: *Valletta*

not won in competitions:
Shalunt
people met on: *Corfu*
things brought home from:
Glassel, Jubones, Anjozorobe
HOME
at BBC Radio studios, birds
that make their: *Waccamaw*
people who'd rather go: *Lowther*
stuff that turns up in your:
Mavesyn Ridware
things that don't look good at:
Jubones
things that happen on the way:
Heanton Punchardon
things that might be at:
Mankinholes
time to go: *Inigonish*
HOOKS
jammy: *Halcro*
picture, things for banging in:
Nogdam End
HOOVER
putting away a: *Lynwilg*
sofas: *Swelling*
under feet: *Hucknall*
HOPEFULNESS
misplaced, of being amusing:
Gaffney
naïve, regarding lunch: *Jeffers*
naïve, regarding tea:
Teigngrace
of finding idiot: *Kibblesworth*
of getting better invitation:
Darvel
HORNS
large, uncomfortable: *Humby*
long, ceremonial: *Hunsingore*
moderate-sized, but
unconcealable: *Huby*
small, Scandinavian:
Oswaldtwistle
HORROR
conversational: *Wigan*
inexpressible: *Maaruig*

HORSES
china, rude: *Barstibley*
understandably irate: *Belding*
HOSTESSES, air: *Ewelme*
HOTELS
clothes ill-advisedly worn in:
Valletta
incredibly dull things in:
Lamlash
mock-Tudor: *Melcombe Regis*
shambolic, clanking: *Bonkle*
HOUSES
dolls': *Tewel*
Opera, spittle in Royal: *Ullapool*
rented: *Delaware*
rubble removal from: *Shottle*
strange, dark: *Islesteps*
strange, noisy: *Whissendine*
things in the cellar of: *Tanvats*
White, amnesiacs in: *Esterhazy*
HUNCHES, foolish, in the theatre:
Totteridge
HUTLERS, clumsy: *Hutlerburn*
HYMNS
pitched at random: *Royston*
pitched too high or low:
Detchant

I

ICE, octogenarians under the:
Wivenhoe
IDEA
having a better: *Ferfer*
not having the faintest: *Epsom,
Osbaston*
very much his own: *Brough
Sowerby*
IDENTITY CARDS, left at home:
Margate
IDIOTS
roaring, pretentious: *Haugham*
ludicrous, deluded:
Kibblesworth

IMPLEMENTS
curious, horticultural: *Haxby*
useless: *Ipplepen*
wooden, silly: *Ibstock*
INCOME TAX, impossibility of
understanding: *Swanibost*
INFANTS, small, naked, comical:
Barstibley
INFORMATIVE, disinclined to be:
Clixby
INKLINGS, tiny, stomach-
curdling: *Ely*
INTERESTING
how: *Nome*
mildly: *Scugog*
temporarily: *Glassel*
than you, someone more:
Sconser
than your newspaper, more:
Corfe
INTERVAL
eight-month: *Peterculter*
theatre bars in the: *Tabley
Superior*
INTO EACH OTHER
bumping: *Droitwich*
things that go: *Toronto*
INVITATIONS
obligatory: *Oughterby*
waited for: *Darvel*
ITEMS
nasal, airborne: *Scronkey*
prune-like, waterlogged:
Dewlish
sticky, clammy: *Belper*
sticky, furry: *Silloth*
thin, circular, meaty: *Shanklin*

J

JACKETS
dust: *Pulverbatch*
hairy, stained: *Bradford*
hideous casual: *Saffron Walden*

loud check: *Louth*
not quite long enough: *Stebbing*
things found in: *Nupend*

JAM
canteen, semi-delicious
ingredients of: *Masberry*
jars, coverings for: *Jid*
used for fastening clothes:
Halcro

JOGGING, suicide by means of:
Kingston Bagpuise

JOHNNIES, rubber: *Sneem,
Phillack*

JOKES
decreasingly funny: *Gignog*
early warnings of ends of:
Pontybodkin
length of: *Gildersome*
medieval, practical: *Araglin*
mild for vicars: *Bude*
practical, spectacular: *Banteer*
technically inept: *Jofane*
told to wrong audience:
Saucillo
well-received: *Smyrna*

JUDGES, things they have to put
up with: *Dockery, Glazeley*

K

KEYS
car, endless inability to find:
Dalfibble
useless bunches of: *Burton
Coggles*

KILTS, hoary old gags about:
Glenwhilly

KINDNESS, unconvincing forms
of: *Frutal*

KISS
musical accompaniment to:
Kabwum
performed while chewing gum:
Oystermouth

KITCHENS
incomprehensible technology
in: *Pingaring*
walls of: *Smearisary*

KNEES
soreness of due to rock and
roll: *Dattuck*
soreness of due to sex: *Bures*

KNIGHTS
frequent: *Dubbo*
teased: *Araglin*
wet: *Bealings*

KNIVES
fish, other uses for: *Botswana*
muddled up with forks:
Fentonadle

KNOBS
medium-size: *Belper*
pointless, stony: *Plympton*

KNOTS
in handkerchiefs: *Sidcup*
intricate: *Kanturk*

L

LADIES, cleaning: *Clabby*

LAUGHTER
awkward absence of:
Umberleigh
hearty, false: *York*
loyal: *Princes Risborough*
tactical: *Swanage*

LAVATORIES
hats in downstairs: *Tweedsmuir*
insufficient willy-waggling in:
Piddletrenthide, Botley
juvenile behaviour in:
Tincleton
keenness to visit: *Iping*
misleading stains acquired in:
Botley
panic preceding visits to: *Great
Wakering*
search for unstained: *Wyoming*

things you shouldn't be doing
in: *Skulamus*
unsightly: *Klosters*
LAWNMOWERS, frustrated:
Trispen
LEATHERY FLAPPING BITS:
Luppitt
LEEDS, hotels in: *Absecon*
LEGS
extremely unwelcome things
up: *Scrabster*
false, improvised: *Ludlow*
things not underneath: *High
Limerigg*
things underneath: *Hucknall*
unwelcome things down:
Wimbledon
unwelcome things on: *Polloch*
unwelcome things up: *Affpuddle*
useless: *Clun*
welcome things up: *Burwash*
LETTERS
deceptively enticing:
Hugglescote
French: *Phillack, Sneem*
important: *Morangie*
incomprehensible: *Dalderby*
LICKING, of envelopes: *Scramoge*
LIDS
noises caused by: *Balzan*
things immediately beneath: *Jid*
useless for putting on things,
apparently antique: *Lydd*
LIFE
state of your: *Shimpling*
the British Way of: *Botcherby*
the facts of: *Ambleside*
uneventfulness of: *Chimkent*
LIFTS
heavy breathing in: *Burbage*
misuse of by weeds: *Nybster*
silence in: *Emsworth*
LIGHTBULBS
dazedness caused by: *Lampung*
needing to be disposed of: *Fring*

problems of disposing of: *Clathy*
LIMP
arm, thespian: *Oundle*
bogus, sporting: *Hoddlesdon*
bread: *Yate*
LINES, wavy: *Ghent*
LITERARY CRITICS: *Ripon*
LOAVES, curious-shaped:
Bradworthy
LOBBY, great oafs screeching in
the: *Haugham*
LOOKS
frosty: *Gartness*
lecherous: *Frosses*
polite, angry: *Evercreech*
superior, at shoes: *Dubuque*
superior, in theatre: *Tabley
Superior*
warning: *Balemartine*
wistful, unexplained: *Foping*
LOST
in any one of a number of
places: *Kelling*
in the grass: *Rimbey*
in the mists of history:
Hutlerburn
in the photocopier: *Dufton*
objects than turn up: *Winkley*
perpetually: *Dalfibble*
quickly becoming: *Brindle*
LOUDNESS
of apologies: *Hickling*
of declaimed opinions: *Prague*
of gurgling: *Pitlochry*
of jacket: *Louth*
of nocturnal noises: *Taroom,
Bonkle*
of voice: *Rufforth, Yarmouth,
Haugham, Lulworth*
LOVERS, used up by, Germaine
Greer: *Shrivenham*
LOUNGES, cocktail: *Melcombe
Regis*
LOVE, unrequited: *Lydiard
Tregoze*

[207]

LUGGAGE
economical with: *Nuncargate*
ill-behaved: *Adlestrop*

LUMPS
agricultural, aromatic: *Jarrow*
awkward, in trousers: *Stebbing*
cardboard, useful: *Ludlow*
disgusting, attached to face:
Kirby
dull, in suitcase: *Glassel*
edible, steaming, irremovable:
Glossop
gristly, acrid: *Grimsby*
gummy, shapeless: *Papcastle*
powdery, floating: *Pages*
small, awkward, dangerous:
Fraddam
small, nasal: *Peebles*
tiny, in swimming trunks:
Lubcroy
unwelcome, nocturnal, in front:
Humby
unwelcome, nocturnal,
underneath: *Tolob*
unwelcome, urban, all over:
Burlingjobb
urban, overhead and underfoot:
Bromsgrove
useless, that stick out: *Zod*,
Huby

M

MAD, you don't have to be, etc:
Snitterfield
MADMEN, departed, in toasters:
Throckmorton
MAKE UP
kiss and: *Manitoba*
lopsided: *Wollondilly*
MANHOLES, open, amusing:
Frimley
MANOEUVRES, awkward,
leaping: *Hobbs Cross*

MAPS, road: *Kalami*
MARGARINE: *Darenth*
MARKETS, super: *Duggleby*,
Flimby, Motspur, Boscastle
MATS, small, sopping: *Listowel*
MATTER, gaseous: *Eriboll*
MATTRESSES
banana-shaped: *Baumber*
enormous, muscular:
Harbledown
MAYBE, meaning no: *Yesnaby*
MEALS
arguments about where to
have: *Lowther*
arguments at the end of:
Bodmin
hopelessly over optimistic:
Jeffers
light, nutritious, for busy
playwrights: *Cresbard*
noises after: *Poona*
things they come in: *Wubin*
to avoid: *Skannerup*
MEANINGLESS
components, small: *Pimlico*
holes in brogues: *Tockholes*
letters to editor: *Dalderby*
noises, distant: *Amersham*
smiles, shiny: *Ewelme*
MEASURE OF LUMINOSITY:
Blean
MEASURES OF DISTANCE
car parks: *Nad*
sheep: *Sheppey*
trousers: *Malibu*
tubes: *Frant*
MEASURES OF TIME
art galleries: *Frolesworth*
lifts: *Emsworth*
mobile phone shops:
Ainsworth
MEAT, ghastly surprises in:
Aigburth
MEDALLIONS, gold:
Herstmonceux

MEMORY
attempts to prod the, into some
kind of action: *Memus*
difficulty of getting things to
lodge in the: *Dinder*
frustrating behaviour of: *Cafu,
Fiunary*
loss of in kitchen: *Woking*
loss of in White House:
Esterhazy
loss of re bruises: *Ampus*
MEN
dismal, pedantic, little: *Benburb*
pathetic, deluded, little:
Brough Sowerby
myopic, dangerous, little: *Low
Eggborough*
MENUS
at the end of meal, people who
reach for: *Scranton*
bits you can remember of:
Kenilworth
Muslim: *Albuquerque*
MERCILESS BOILING: *Cong*
MERRY-GO-ROUNDS: *Adrigole*
MID-PEE, pulling the chain in:
Tincleton
MIDDLE
aged coloraturas: *Ullingswick*
aged ladies: *Lossiemouth*
aged, balding: *Ugglebarnby*
aged, desperate: *Papigochic*
Ages, trousers worn in:
Goosecruives
class: *Pitroddie*
of night: *Balzan, Lampung*
of nowhere, hairs found in:
Albacete
of perusal: *Peru*
of Scottish folk song: *Lochranza*
MILK JUGS, unnecessary
numbers of: *Upottery*
MISTAKES
horrifying, too drunk to avoid:
Hagnaby

horrifying, unavoidable: *Wigan*
MOATS: *Bealings*
MOBILE PHONES: problems
buying: *Ainsworth, Hotagen*
MODESTY, false: *Simprim*
MOMENTS
awful: *Umberleigh*
deeply embarrassing: *Lulworth*
utterly pant-wetting: *Wembley*
MONASTERIES: *Corstorphine*
MOODS
anti-vegetative: *Hewish*
irrational: *Cranleigh*
of deep irritation: *Corriecravie*
peevish, sofa-destroying:
Pollatomish
wavily-depicted: *Ghent*
MOORS: *Luffness, Luffenham,
Slogarie*
MORNING
after a bagpipe playing contest:
Spittal of Glenshee
after a party: *Picklenash, Silloth*
bits of you waking up in the:
Tingewick
cheerfulness in the: *Spreakley*
five o'clock in the: *Bonkle*
horrid awakening in the:
Maaruig
nasty shock in the: *Hagnaby*
stiff and achey in the: *Liniclate*
surprising appearance in the:
Sheepy Magna
three o'clock in the: *Burslem*
time off in the: *Slipchitsy*
twenty past nine in the:
Framlingham
two o'clock in the: *Pott Shrigley*
MORON, not wanting to be
thought a: *Frolesworth*
MORSELS, small prominent,
repulsive: *Kirby*
MOTORBIKES
feeling of new: *Nempnett
Thrubwell*

involuntary impersonation of:
Berepper

MOTORWAYS
not to be confused with
madmen on: *Gastard*
sudden outbreaks of cones on:
Skagway
sudden outbreaks of
law-abiding behaviour on:
Grimbister
sudden outbreaks of lunch on:
Strassgang
sudden outbreaks of reckless
joyfulness on: *Jalingo*

MOUSSAKA, stout pubes in:
Scroggs

MOVEMENTS
bowel: *Glororum*
fishlike: *Gipping*
flabby: *Humber*
futile, at Post Offices: *Stoke
Poges*
futile, at waiters: *Epping*
futile, in own house: *Kelling*
vague, manual, searching:
Scosthrop
waggling, artistic: *Llanelli*

MUMBLES, deliberate:
Inverkeithing

MURMANSK, things that
shouldn't be in: *Glentaggart*

MUSH, dehydrated: *Pott Shrigley*

MUSIC
rendered weepy by old:
Cahors
simple, played badly: *Dinsdale*

N

'N': *Nacton*

NAMES
being cute with: *Ocilla, Cheb*
cheating with: *Aalst*
execrable: *Drebley*

forgetting of: *Golant,
Inverkeithing*
loves that dare not speak their:
Lyminster
sudden reconsidering of: *Abert*

NAP
conditions in which you should
try to have a: *Duntish, Hynish,
Cranleigh*
limbs having a: *Clun*
things brushed against the:
Nith

NEEDLES
conversations that are largely
concerned with: *Gussage*
things that won't go through
the eye of: *Vidlin*

NEW YORK
cluelessness in: *Lackawanna*
employment opportunities in:
Steenhuffel

NEWS, astounding: *Jawcraig*

NEWSPAPER
cuttings, comical: *Snitter*
fascination of someone else's:
Corfe
opinions gleaned from: *Macroy*
racks, bewildering fascination
with: *Condover*

NIGHT
dazedness during: *Lampung*
noises during: *Balzan,
Whissendine, Bonkle, Boinka*
things purloined during:
Ambatolampy

NIPPLES, high profile: *Budby*

NITWITS, great steaming:
Duggleby

NO, expressed as yes: *Yesnaby*

NODS
surly, from behind hedge:
Todber
thoughtful, vacant: *Dinder*

NODULES
plastic melted: *Stutton*

rubber: *Pimperne*

Noises
  bodily, benign: *Bepton*
  bubbling and inopportune:
  Tumby
  burbling and nocturnal: *Bonkle*
  discreet but unwelcome: *Affcot*
  distant and meaningless:
  Amersham
  grunting and considerate:
  Horton-cum-Studley
  gurgling and milky: *Pitlochry*
  gushing and cooing: *Oshkosh*
  humming and grinding:
  Burleston
  humming and groaning:
  Milwaukee
  loud and clattering:
  Clackmannan
  loud and deafening: *Balzan*
  loud and embarrassing: *Berepper*
  loud and informative: *Taroom*
  loud and rattling: *Hoggeston*
  loud and revolving: *Cairo*
  minuscule, worrying: *Fring*
  mumbling, uninterested:
  Nazeing
  nocturnal, interminable:
  Framlingham
  nocturnal, intermittent:
  Whissendine
  painful and squeaky:
  Skibbereen
  post-prandial: *Poona*
  quiet and rubbery: *Tampa*
  resounding from clifftops:
  Craboon
  screeching, Celtic: *Lochranza*
  screeching, infantile:
  Caarnduncan
  squeaky, nylonish: *Screeb*
  tat-tatting and satisfying:
  Ibstock
  ticketatacketaticketting:
  Seattle
  ticketatacktackatucka-
  ticketting: *Trantlemore*
  triumphant and slappy: *Beppu*
  trumpeting, hippopotamoid:
  Brampton
  warm and underwater: *Budle*
  whiffling, in lifts: *Burbage*
  whirring and chuntering:
  Ipswich

Norris, Chuck: *Duncraggon*

Noses
  adornments to: *Botolphs*
  bleeding: *Burton Coggles*
  erstwhile contents of:
  Longniddry
  fascinating items in:
  Massachusetts
  ill-equipped to deal with
  runny: *Hankate*
  noises made with: *Burbage*
  things which are ejected from:
  Scurlage
  things which come down from:
  Des Moines
  things which stretch a long way
  from: *Coilantogle*
  tools for stuffing into:
  Botusfleming

Nozzles, aircraft, strange
  powers over: *Ventnor*

Numbers
  lost: *Staplow*
  wrong, for any given purpose:
  Pleven
  wrong, of potatoes: *Peoria*
  wrong, or so he claims:
  Kurdistan

Nerds
  conferences for unwanted,
  Absecon
  excited: *Hugglescote*
  incredible little: *Corfu*
  lanky, Scandinavian: *Ullock*
  piddling, in your lavatory:
  Tincleton

preeping: *Widdicombe*
tittering, white-collar: *Snitterby*

O

OBJECTS
banana-shaped: *Baumber*
bloody-minded: *Ardslignish*
clammy, inedible: *Amlwch*
contented stares at: *Dallow,
Skellow*
creatively misapplied: *Botswana*
dangerously misleading: *Pymble*
deformed: *Duddo*
elephantine: *Clackmannan*
fantastically dull: *Lamlash*
flimsy, intriguing: *Corfu*
frilly: *Ossett*
heavy, with toes on: *Clun*
hidden, pointed: *Gilgit*
hideous, shelfbound: *Delaware*
hitherto unnamed: *Liff*
horrible, roomy: *Mapledurham*
innocent, repeatedly hit: *Ashdod*
Kenyan: *Jubones*
long-handled: *Botusfleming*
lost, found again: *Winkley*
massive, wooden, airborne:
Camer
plastic, pretentious: *Brumby*
sticky, jam-infested: *Halcro*
sticky, permanent: *Dipple*
sticky, wooden: *Cotterstock*
strange, culinary: *Cong*
that don't fool anyone: *Zeerust*
tiny, disgusting: *Chipping
Ongar*
tiny, pointless: *Didcot*
twelve, baffling: *Cowcaddens*
unappealing, lonely: *Brymbo*
wet, cold, enormous: *Trewoofe*
with bumps on: *Bolsover*
with holes in, artistic:
Bromsgrove, Dalrymple

OFFICERS, retired, army, raving:
Pant-y-Wacco
OFFICES
comical cuttings on walls of:
Snitter
fat chance of getting anything
to work properly in: *Podebrady*
lost pieces of paper in: *Dufton*
managers who hide in their:
Harmanger
people who decorate: *Clovis,
Snitterby*
resentful people in: *Brough
Sowerby*
scapegoats in: *Bickerstaffe*
OFFICIALS
people who become: *Benburb*
who make your life a misery:
Margate
OLDS
bounding, refrigerated, eighty-
year-: *Wivenhoe*
cringe-making, fourteen-year-:
Cheb
on heat, sixteen-year-: *Frosses*
sweating, forty-year-: *Kingston
Bagpuise*
ON, trying it: *Brabant*
OOZE, yellow: *Clonmult*
OPINIONS
confident, wrong: *Macroy*
hard to tolerate: *Chaling*
that taxi-drivers wish to
share with you: *Watendlath,
Crieff*
unasked-for, reverend: *Dean
Funes*
ORCHESTRA PITS, spittle in:
Ullapool
ORCHESTRAS
conducted from the audience:
Thrumster
which spit a lot: *Ullapool*
ORGASM, MULTIPLE: *Papworth
Everard*

ORNAMENTS, misapplied:
Bishop's Caundle
wooden: *Tuamgraney*
OVERALLS, inky: *Hibbing*

P

PAGE
last, of book: *Beppu*
last, of document, left in
photocopier: *Dufton*
single, blithering: *Clackavoid*
PAIN AND SHAME: *Yonkers*
PAINS, sudden: *Acle*
PAINT, smudges, expensive:
Dalrymple
PAINTBRUSHES, cheap: *Aith*
PAINT-STIRRERS: *Cotterstock*
PANGS, terrible: *Lydiard Tregoze*
PANIC
in airport: *Hever*
in corridor: *Ditherington*
in lavatory: *Great Wakering*
PAPER
barely soiled toilet: *Riber*
silver, against teeth: *Tingrith*
tangled, spinning: *Strelley*
under lid: *Jid*
PARENTS
attempts to mislead: *Shimpling*
embarrassed: *Sneem*
god: *Urchfont*
parties given by: *Frosses*
PARTICLES, nasal: *Massachusetts*
PARTIES
adventurous behaviour at:
Hallspill
crud under sofas after: *Silloth*
deposits acquired at curious
dinner: *Sutton and Cheam*
dreadful guests at: *Nubbock,
Oughterby*
frosty glances at dinner:
Inigonish

heated recriminations after:
Heanton Punchardon
irritatingly successful people
at: *Draffan, Offord Darcy*
people to avoid at: *East
Wittering, West Wittering*
political: *Firebag*
steamy, teenage: *Frosses*
things drunk in desperation at
end of: *Aasleagh*
things found in lager cans at
the end of: *Slumbay*
things found in wine glasses
after: *Picklenash*
things removed from rooms
before: *Spokane*
welcome departures from:
Nubbock
women's conversational
exclusiveness at: *Flums*
PARTS, private, had by dog for
lunch: *Scorrier*
PATCHES
wet, under bottom: *Hobbs Cross*
wet, underarm: *Pitsligo*
PAVING STONES: *Affpuddle*
PEBBLES, wet, shiny: *Glassel*
PEDANTS: *Ainderby Quernhow*
PEE
foot-tingling sensations caused
by: *Gilling*
inability to do with audience
present: *Kettleness*
PELLETS, unmentionable:
Peebles
PENCIL SHARPENINGS, giant:
Blitterlees
PENISES
embarrassingly visible:
Stebbing
embarrassingly visible,
useless: *Huby*
hard-working: *Papworth Everard*
inexpertly rendered likenesses
of: *Skrubburdnut*

injuries to: *Minchinhampton*
interested: *Tingewick*
lawn-sprinkling mode of: *Spuzzum*
moist: *Wetwang*
obstinate: *Humby*
played with: *Southwick*, *Sloinge*
politely washed: *Paradip*
regularly moved about: *Grobister*
tent-supporting: *Visby*

PENS
lack of: *Aynho*
uselessness of: *Kilvaxter*

PEOPLE
boring, pairs of: *Mimbridge*
cringing, irritating: *Greeley*
frantic, disorganized: *Worksop*
irritatingly acquiescent: *Dunino*
irritatingly non-acquiescent: *Nindigully*
large groups of helpful grunting: *Horton-cum-Studley*
large groups of miserly: *Bodmin*
medium-sized clumps of enraged: *Dolgellau*
neat old: *Pingandy*
niggling: *Scranton*
reassuring: *Lemvig*
reliably unreliable: *Marytavy*
small families of horrible: *Molesby*
small groups of whiffling: *Burbage*
smooth greedy: *Winston-Salem*
suspiciously motivated: *Frutal*
underprivileged; leg-wise: *Wigan*
unshaven, maddening: *Draffan*
vast, wobble-cheeked: *Humber*
who give themselves the biggest slice: *Finuge*
who should not be allowed near a piano: *Dinsdale*
wrong-sized groups of: *Lampeter*
you don't want to talk to again: *Staplow*

PERPETUITY, in: *Cotterstock*

PHOTOGRAPHS
passport, amusement caused by: *Happas*
passport, expressions worn in: *Banff*

PIANO
moving: *Nundle*
people who should on no account be allowed near a: *Dinsdale*

PICNIC SPOTS
disappointing: *Munderfield*
infested with wasps: *Swaffham Bulbeck*

PIGS, matching: *Tibshelf*

PILES, unstable: *Boscastle*

PILLOWS
clean: *Abilene*
damp: *Sompting*

PIMPLES, volcanic: *Bilbster*

PINS
dangerous: *Acle*
safety: *Lubcroy*

PIPERS: *Lochranza*

PIPES, things hit by: *Ashdod*

PLACES, safe: *Fiunary*

PLANTS
artificial, diseased: *Breckles*
sentenced to death: *Lutton Gowts*
thwacking at: *Hewish*

PLASTER, torn off skin: *Wike*

PLEASURE, idiosyncratic, revolting: *Glarorum*

PLUGS, bath: *Dillytop*, *Twomileborris*

PLUMBERS
could do with a visit from some: *Bonkle*

ignorance of whereabouts of:
Suckley Knowl

PLUMBING NOISES: *Bonkle*

POCKETS
omnivorous: *Nantucket*
public displays of searching:
Ardelve
upholstered: *Hassop*

POINTS, sound made by trains
crossing: *Trantlemore*

POLES, strong desire to grasp:
Abercrave

POLICE
motorway snarl-ups caused by:
Grimbister
motorway snarl-ups eased by:
Jalingo
the Leith: *Tolstachaolais*
what passes for politeness
amongst the: *Surby*

POLICEMEN, skin of: *Melton
Constable*

POLITICIANS
rabid, left-wing, rich:
Quedgeley
ridiculous, furry-hatted:
Glinsk

POLITICS
sole contribution to: *Spoffard*
tiresome: *Firebag*

POLTERGEISTS, resident in car:
Worgret

POODLES, glass: *Tibshelf*

PORNOGRAPHY, the making of:
Papworth Everard

POSITIONS, switches which seem
to be off in both: *Ockle*

POTATOES
fear of: *Peoria*
misshapen: *Duddo*

POUCHES
small, designer, condom-
containing: *Phillack*
small, humorous: *Glenwhilly*

POULTRY-KEEPERS: *Goosecruives*

PRATS, overdressed,
incompetent: *Kitmurvy*

PREFACES: *Querrin*

PRETENCES
absurd: *Dogdyke*
ingratiating: *Puning*
intellectual: *Bathel*
proud: *Prungle*
seasonal: *Fulking*

PRICES
gin: *Le Touquet*
property: *Munster*

PROBLEMS
of disposing of lightbulbs:
Clathy
of putting on sweater: *Hessle*

PRONGS
bent: *Bromsgrove*
concealed: *Hadzor*
clogged with sludge: *Henstridge*
truncated: *Baldock*

PRUNE-LIKE EXTREMITIES:
Dewlish

PUBS
berks in: *Louth, Boothby Graffoe*
passing time of day in: *Todding*
table hoggers in: *Stody*
to open, waiting for the:
Luffenham

PUDDINGS, miserable: *Nutbourne*

PUDDLES
exterior: *Burwash, Affpuddle*
interior: *Goole, Sketty*

PUNISHMENT, capital, in
schools: *Little Urswick*

PURPOSE, unfathomable: *Haxby*

PUS, scarlet: *Buldoo*

PUSH TAPS, embarrassment
caused by: *Botley*

PUSHY, people who are: *Brabant*

PYJAMAS
comforting: *Lambarene*
Muslim: *Albuquerque*

PYRAMIDS, metallic: *Boscastle*

Q

QUESTIONS
expecting answers: *Nome*
not expecting answers: *Spurger*
not leaving room for answers:
Ainderby Steeple
QUEUES: *Duggleby, Evercreech,
Foindle, Twomileborris*

R

RACES, three-legged: *Shifnal*
RADIO
boring, high-brow: *Meuse*
boring, low-brow: *Burslem*
boring, middle-brow:
Blandford Forum
strange tropical birds on the:
Waccamaw
RAINCOATS
expensive: *Trossachs*
porous: *Plenmeller*
RATTLING, senseless: *Amersham*
REACTIONS, chemical,
unedifying: *Bradford*
REALIZATIONS
embarrassing: *Gammersgill,
Hidcote Bartram*
irritating: *Tooting Bec*
lurching: *Bedfont*
sudden: *Duleek, Dunboyne*
REASONS
for clipping things, no
apparent: *Didcot*
for designing bath plug, no
accountable: *Dillytop*
for naming things, no known:
Sadberge
for sleeping with people,
obscure: *Randers*
for spray in your mouth,
unknown: *Skoonspruit*

for staring at something, no
particular: *Dallow*
REASSURANCE
much needed: *Godalming*
spurious: *Old Cassop*
RECEPTION
chilly: *Saucillo*
not very good: *Gweek*
RELATIONSHIPS
unresolved: *Badachonacher*
wish to sort out other people's:
Canudos
RELEVANT
only slightly: *Juwain*
surprisingly: *Gress*
RELISH TRAYS: *Clonmult,
Sadberge, Buldoo*
RELUCTANCE
feigned, easily overcome: *Climpy*
feigned, very easily overcome:
Alcoy
REMARKS
calculated, crowd-pleasing:
Firebag
own, rather amusing, unheard:
Dorchester, Umberleigh
pompous, hypocritical, clichéd:
Reculver
stoicism in the face of
wounding: *Calicut*
REMOVALS
non-furniture: *Dipple, Grimsby,
Rickling, Spokane, Tolob,
Watendlath, Botusfleming, Crail*
piano: *Nundle*
REQUESTS, whining, unwelcome:
Quall
RESTAURANTS
embarrassing manual
behaviour in: *Ardentinny*
embarrassing vocal behaviour
in: *Haugham*
perverse behaviour in: *Kowloon*
REVELATIONS, personal, with
stomach-rumble: *Tumby*

RICHARD III: *Oundle*
RIGHTS
   ancient, pebbly: *Pevensey*
   ancient, with midgets:
     Forsinain
   telling lefts from: *Memus, Noak*
     Hoak
RIPPING, of skin: *Wike*
ROADS, signposting of: *Botcherby*
ROCK, small pieces of,
   apparently limitless quantities
   of: *Crail*
ROLLS, sausage, stuff you
   wouldn't even find in: *Gruids*
ROUND
   but don't come off, things that
     go: *Slettnut*
   but shouldn't, things that go:
     Strelley
   things that don't go: *Adrigole,*
     Motspur
   things that go: *Hextable*
ROUSTABOUTS, TEXAN: *Esher*
ROWING, accidents while:
   Anantnag
RUBBERS
   noises made by: *Tampa*
   places for keeping: *Phillack*
   you didn't want to be asked
   about: *Sneem*
RUBBISH, vital, in dustcart:
   Nottage
RUCKSACKS: *York*
RUGS, horseshoe-shaped, fluffy:
   Luton
RULERS, noises made by: *Thrupp*
RUNS, token: *Sturry*
RYVITA, consistency of: *Naples*

S

SACHETS, impenetrable:
   Naugatuck
SACKING: *Tillicoultry*

SAFE PLACES: *Fiunary*
SALAMI: *Shanklin*
SANDWICHES
   bacon: *Beccles*
   in London: *Darenth*
   on trains: *Amlwch*
SARONG, appearing in lobby
   wearing a: *Valletta*
SAUCEPANS
   almost but not quite spotless:
     Radlett
   chocolate-filled: *Abinger*
SAUNTERS, carefree: *Frimley*
SAUSAGES
   in rolls: *Gruids*
   stuff to smear on: *Patney*
   twisted: *Kerry*
SCABS, amorous: *Bures*
SCHOOLTEACHERS: *Bradford*
SCISSORS
   looking for: *Scosthrop*
   other uses for: *Nogdam End*
SCONES: *Pudsey*
SCRIBBLES: *Screggan*
SEASIDE, by the, firmly locked in
   car: *Molesby*
SEATS
   aircraft: *Rochester*
   lavatory: *Luton*
SECRET
   deliberately badly kept:
     Marytavy
   supposed to be, but who are
   you trying to kid?: *Tukituki*
SECRETIONS, in hamburger
   joints: *Clonmult*
SELF-KNOWLEDGE, serene,
   completely wrong: *Solent*
SELLOTAPE: *Ardslignish, Pimlico*
SENSATIONS, lurching: *Bedford*
SENTENCES, finishing other
   people's: *Happle*
SERVICES
   church: *Royston, Detchant*
   monastic: *Corstorphine*

SEVEN
miles of concealed moorland: *Slogarie*

SEX
bothersome interruptions of: *Humby*
could probably do with some: *Pollatomish*
enjoyed by other people: *Boinka*
ill-kept secrets about: *Tukituki*
messes caused by: *Hobbs Cross, Bedfont*
minor injuries sustained during: *Bures*
nasty shocks after: *Hagnaby*
nasty shocks before: *Wartnaby*
people who want: *Visby, Low Ardwello*
things that put you off the whole idea of: *Hextable*
uncertain about: *Libode*

SHADES OF GREEN
domestic: *Gretna Green*
institutional: *Frating Green*
things that clearly should not be included among: *Wasp Green*

SHAGGED OUT: *Swanibost*

SHAKESPEARE
working lunches prepared for: *Cresbard*

SHAVING: *Hathersage*

SHEDS
nuclear: *Low Eggborough*
potting: *Haxby*
tool: *Cotterstock*

SHEEP
mysterious complaints of: *Jawcraig*
woolly charm of in distance: *Sheppey*

SHEETS
bloody awful, nylon: *Brecon*
bottom: *Baumber, Bedfont*

SHELVES

hideous stuff on: *Delaware, Tibshelf*
improvised chess pieces found on: *Bishop's Caundle*

SHIFTING, anxious: *Iping*

SHINGLE, collectors of: *Pevensey*

SHIRTS
beer down: *Tulsa*
damp: *Wedderlairs*
open to waist: *Herstmonceux*
stabbing: *Acle*

SHOES
bits that hang off: *Luppitt*
perforations in: *Tockholes*
wrong sort of: *Dubuque*

SHOPS
absent companions who turn up in: *Flagler*
dress: *Dolgellau*
maddening: *Ainsworth*
electrical goods, idiot: *Kibblesworth*
with stupid names: *Drebley*

SHOUTING AT FOREIGNERS: *Yarmouth*

SHOWERS, agonizing: *Alltami*

SICK
feeling in throat after being: *Gulberwick*
off wrong side of boat: *Silesia*

SIDE
things on the other: *Quenby*
things that stick out the: *Aith*
things written on the: *Dorridge*

SIDEBURNS, extensive, scrofulous: *Galashiels*

SIGNPOSTS, pathetic attempt at proper: *Botcherby*

SIGNS, to be taken seriously: *Belding*

SILENCES, ghastly: *Lulworth*

SINGERS
awful: *Royston*
carol, hiding from: *Fulking*
wailing: *Lochranza*

SINGLE
and proud of it, or so they
claim: *Prungle*
desire to see people stop being:
Canudos
hair: *Albacete*
men who are too groovy to
dance: *Peening Quarter*
SIX TIMES BEFORE, stories
heard: *Smarden*
SIXTEEN
-stone men on last legs:
Kingston Bagpuise
-year-olds on heat: *Frosses*
SKIING: *Zeal Monachorum*
SKILLS
bath-filling: *Alltami*
cowardly: *Corriecravie*
loaf-naming: *Bradworthy*
revolting: *Oystermouth*
useless as it turns out: *Aboyne*
SKIN
flaps of: *Scopwick*
twists of: *Kerry*
expanses of: *Bogue*
SLEEP
larcenous behaviour during:
Ambatolampy
muck in eyes after: *Mugeary*
people with whom you're not
sure if you want to: *Libode*
things which might help you
get to: *Burslem*
things which prevent
you getting to: *Burleston,
Framlingham*
things which interrupt your:
Lostwithiel, Dunster
things which shouldn't have
gone to: *Clun*
SLIMMING, feeble dishonest shot
at: *Berkhamsted*
SLOBS
complete: *Snover*
lazy: *Abinger*

SLUDGE
brittle: *Cromarty*
moist: *Eads*
SMELLS, horrible: *Keele*
SMILES
frozen, horrified: *Sneem*
grim, determined: *Smarden*
shiny, meaningless: *Ewelme*
SMOKING, excuses for: *Brisbane*
SMUTTY POSTCARDS: *Snitterfield*
SNACKS, nasty: *Nantwich*
SNEEZING
failure to: *Amersham*
horribly violent success at:
Scronkey
SNIPPETS, hairy: *Hathersage*
SNOW, wedges of lurking:
Trewoofe
SOAP OPERA, Australian:
Clackavoid
SOCKS
contents of: *Skenfrith*
things that appear above: *Bogue*
SOFA
restlessly plucked at:
Pollatomish
things spotted from: *Chenies*
SOLICITORS
excessively elderly: *Skellister*
fat from Tonbridge: *Valletta*
SONG
misheard lyric of: *Rhymney*
Scottish folk: *Lochranza*
that makes you want to cry:
Cahors
SOPPING, shopping: *Sotterley*
SOUP
exotic, made from moats:
Bealings
packet: *Poges*
splattered: *Papple*
tomato: *Scranton, Tomatin*
SPACE AND TIMELESSNESS:
Hambledon
SPASMS, massive facial: *Jawcraig*

[219]

SPEAKER
deliberately ovation-inducing:
Firebag
guest, absolute drivel
concerning: *Euphrates*
SPEECH
affected: *Pitroddie*
fatuous introduction to:
Euphrates
parts of, crucial, obscured:
Dorchester
SPERM
career-oriented: *Hobarris*
copious quantities of: *Toronto*
marooned, damp: *Hobbs Cross*
marooned, dry: *Bedfont*
SPIT: *Gallipoli*
SPOONFUL
eggy: *Symonds Yat*
not quite a: *Pidney*
SPOTS
bites which could be: *Bauple*
to which you have to remain
rooted: *Vollenhove*
SPRIGS, dangling, colourful:
Chenies
SQUEEZING
cosmetic: *Quabbs*
religious: *Clenchwarton*
SQUIGGLES, financial:
Albuquerque
STAINS
inky: *Hibbing*
Marmite: *Sutton and Cheam*
trousers, own fault:
Piddletrenthide
trousers, not own fault: *Botley*
STAIRCASES, winding:
Harbledown
STAIRS
disappearing: *High Limerigg*
falling down the: *Blean*
STANDING ABOUT: *Lowther*
STANDING AND WONDERING:
Woking

STANDING, ways of: *Ahenny*
STARES
harsh, meaningful: *Kurdistan*
mellow, meaningless: *Dallow*
STATE
disease of deposed heads of:
Patkai Bum
hungover: *Duntish*
of barrister's hair: *Glazeley*
of dress: *Grinstead*
of mind: *Hynish, Pant-y-Wacco*
of respectable ladies:
Richmond
STEPS, small, irrevocable:
Glenties
STEW, ghastly items found in:
Grimsby
STICK
out, things that: *Zod, Stebbing,
Huby, Humby, Loberia*
to the point: *Gress*
to your skin, things that: *Wike*
together, things that shouldn't
but do: *Dipple*
together, things that won't:
Soller, Badachonacher
up, things that: *Visby, Pymble*
STICKS
swiping with: *Hewish*
walking: *Clackmannan*
STOMACHS
lurching sensations in: *Bedfont*
STORIES
endless, repetitive, celebrity:
Boothby Graffoe
humorous, heard before:
Plymouth
humorous, interminable:
Gildersome
STRANGE POWERS OVER
AIRCRAFT NOZZLES: *Ventnor*
STRANGER, than a zebra: *Yebra*
STRANGERS
perfect, bewildering messages
from: *Berriwillock*

[220]

perfect, patronizing remarks
made by: *Maynooth*
perfect, who grab your naughty
bits: *Zagreb*
STREAKS, brown: *Wyoming*
STREETS
cleaning of: *Vancouver*
epiglottises spotted on: *Scugog*
exasperating encounters on:
Vollenhove
STRIPS, grimy: *Torlundy*
STUBBLE
in basin: *Hathersage*
in sandwiches: *Munderfield*
STUMPS, tree: *Baldock*
SUBJECT
declaimed ignorantly upon:
Prague
of property prices: *Munster*
someone to unwelcome
attentions: *Boothby Graffoe*,
Peterculter, *Corfu*
SUBSTANCES
brown, squashy: *Skegness*
green, synthetic: *Halifax*
grey, gummy: *Deal*
ochre, indelicate: *Quabbs*
yellow, dried: *Henstridge*
yellow, squelchy: *Mugeary*
white, flaky: *Skenfrith*
various colours, gushing:
Toronto
SUNBATHING: *Kimmeridge*,
Kettering
SURPRISES
hair-induced: *Albacete*
unpleasant, at public school:
Percyhorner
SUSPICIONS
horrible: *Mankinholes*
of infidelity: *Kurdistan*
SWATTING: *Bursledon*
SWEAT
patches of, enticingly
displayed: *Pitsligo*

patches of, large: *Wedderlairs*
small, moving beads of:
Elsrickle
SWIGS, nasty surprises in:
Slumbay
SWINDON, futile attempts to exit:
Wendens Ambo
SWITCHES, useless: *Ockle*

T

TABLES
antique, priceless, ruined:
Glossop
dressing, cluttered with
garbage: *Boolteens*, *Lamlash*
highly polished antique
rosewood dining: *Glossop*
inexpertly laid: *Fentonadle*
leapt on to: *Pabbay*
not laying: *Nanhoron*
shy behaviour near: *Namber*
things left on kitchen: *Pudsey*
things stuck under wobbly:
Ludlow
TACTICS
diversionary: *Swanage*
thwarted: *Aboyne*
TALKING, unlikelihood of
stopping: *Hove*
TANNOY, half heard: *Hever*
TAPS
foot-operated: *Polbathic*
pointless: *Pocking*
push, trouser-dousing: *Esher*
TARPAULINS: *Flodigarry*
TAXI-DRIVERS: *Fovant*
TAXIS
driven by idiots: *Lackawanna*
hypocrisy resorted to in: *Crieff*
opinions offered in: *Watendlath*
seductive remarks in: *Low
Ardwello*
smell of: *Duluth*

Teaspoon, the ultimate: *Scullet*

Teeth
feelings in: *Tingrith*
food stores between: *Glutt Lodge*
improvised things used to clean between: *Sigglesthorne*
results of cleaning: *Misool*
things that might have been caused by: *Bauple*
unwelcome views of: *Scugog*

Teeth, smiling determinedly through: *Smarden*

Telephone directories, collectors of antique: *Aldclune*

Telephones
embarrassing memory loss when using: *Gammersgill*
inability to get off: *Harpenden*
numbers, misplaced: *Staplow*
suspicious number of wrong numbers when answering: *Kurdistan*
uselessness of: *Ipswich*

Television
afternoons wasted in front of: *Gonnabarn*
celebrity, fat: *Melbury Bubb*
commercials, chuckles at the end of: *Lybster*
interviewers, look inflicted by: *Scridain*
newsreaders, determined not to be embarrassed: *Hosmer*
presenters, tone of voice of: *Tonypandy*
series based on books: *Bathel*
willing to be on: *Sicamous*

Theatre, practices in: *Hickling, Totteridge, Tabley Superior*

Thimbles
conversations that probably touch upon the subject of: *Gussage*
things that aren't: *Pymble*

Things
small, complex: *Uttoxeter*
small, pleasant: *Strubby*
small, worrying: *Exeter*
squirty, for ironing: *Perranzabuloe*
to do: *Worksop*
various: *Sutton and Cheam*

Ties
inelegantly knotted: *Ranfurly*
innate cussedness of: *Clingman's Dome*

Tights, misuse of: *Grinstead*

Tingles
apprehensive: *Ely*
delightful: *Gilling*

Tins
attempts to find things to open: *Scosthrop*
biscuit: *Lindisfarne*
of emulsion, stubborn: *Botswana*
of soup: *Tomatin*
pyramids of: *Boscastle*

Tips, felt: *Scremby*

Toasters
spirits that inhabit: *Throckmorton*
uselessness of: *Yate, Burnt Yates*
work, attempts to make: *Throcking*

Toblerones, consequences of triangular shape of: *Gubblecote*

Toenails, contents of: *Tidpit*

Toes, slime on: *Deal*

Toiletries
misapplied: *Wollondilly*
mixed: *Glud*
rather naughty: *Spruce Knob*

Tongs, silver, for poking Freemasons: *Grimsby*

Tongue
things touched with: *Lingle, Moisie*

[222]

unwelcome glimpses of: *Scugog*
TOWELS, damp: *Wrabness*
TOXIC
  foreshores: *Spinwam*
  soup: *Tomatin*
  waste ground: *Caarnduncan*
TRACTORS, dung-spreading:
  Jarrow
TRAIN
  conversations on: *Jawf*
  departed without one:
  Dunboyne
  impersonation of: *Trantlemore,*
  Seattle
  inedible things on: *Amlwch*
  non-arrival of: *Amersham*
  Royal: *Didcot*
  tickets: *Nantucket*
TREES
  Nigerian: *Masberry*
  stumps of: *Baldock*
TRIMPHONES, impersonation of:
  Widdicombe
TRIPPING OVER CARPET:
  Thurnby
TROLLEYS, rogue: *Motspur*
TROUSERS
  elderly: *Broats*
  inflatable: *Huby*
  roguish: *Minchinhampton*
  soaking: *Esher*
  stained: *Botley, Piddletrenthide*
  too long: *Malibu*
  wooden: *Goosecruives*
  wrong pair of: *Duggleby*
TROUTS, fierce old: *Baughurst*
TRUCKS, street-cleaning:
  Vancouver
TRUNKS, swimming: *Lubcroy*
TRUTH, palpable: *Hoff*
TUBES
  in London: *Amersham,*
  Chicago
  in meat: *Aigburth*
  in spring: *Pitsligo*

TUBS, impenetrable: *Polloch*
TUMMIES
  nasty feelings in pits of: *Ely*
  pregnant: *Stowting*
  sounds that emanate from:
  Tumby
TURDS
  (dog) comely, well-
  proportioned: *Joliette*
  (dog) small, but still nasty:
  Bromsgrove
  thick as your wrist: *Laxobigging*
TURN-UPS, fertile: *Huttoft*
TWATS, annoying: *Thrumster*
TWEEZERS, difficulty with:
  Hadweenzic
TWERPS, bicycle-oriented:
  Wormelow Tump
TWITCHING, uncontrollable: *West*
  Wittering
TYPO, Welsh: *Maentwrog*

U

UMBRELLA STANDS:
  Clackmannan
UMBRELLAS
  absent when needed: *Sotterley,*
  Plenmeller
  in drinks, stupid little: *Limassol*
  things that aren't: *Dunolly*
UNDERBLANKETS, lumpy: *Tolob*
UNDERCLOTHES, bestrewn:
  Adlestrop
UNDERPANT, half an: *Scrabby*
UNDERPANTS
  floorbound: *Slobozia*
  incomplete: *Scrabby*
UNDRESSING
  happily watching other people:
  Beaulieu Hill
  unhappily watching other
  people: *Wartnaby*
URGES, violent: *Kent*

small hours of the night, things
that go bang in the: *Balzan*
small hours of the night, things
that gurgle in the: *Bonkle*

WEE-WEE
broad jets of: *Spuzzum*
humorous, artificial: *Barstibley*
inopportune moment to have to
have a: *Humby*
strategies for having a: *Lower
Peover*

WEEK, day of, deliberate
ignorance of: *Abligo*

WELSH RAREBIT, growth on:
Eriboll

WHITEBAIT, pieces of chewed,
flying: *Satterthwaite*

WILLIES, insufficiently waggled:
Piddletrenthide, Botley

WIND, GONE WITH THE:
Epworth

WINDCHEATERS: *Savernake*

WING
left: *Quedgeley*
right: *Firebag*

WIPERS, windscreen: *Memphis*

WISDOM, NORMAN: *Frimley*

WOOLF, VIRGINIA: *York*

WORDS
deceptive: *Nossob*
Eskimo: *Anantnag*
hatefulness of certain:
Quoyness
Indonesian, relaxed: *Toodyay*
people who bang on about:
Ainderby Quernhow

WORKMAN
cleavage in bottom of: *Ravenna*
fraudulent: *Podebrady*

WOUNDS
doubtful: *Hoddlesdon*
on elbows: *Bures*

WRONG
camera: *Hosmer*
gone terribly: *Ely*
place, heart in the: *Willimantic*
things you're in a mind to get:
Hynish

Y

YAWNS
badly suppressed: *Wawne*
one who: *Lolland*
things that produce a lot of:
Dolgellau, Rigolet

YEARNINGS
batty: *Abercrave*
nostalgic: *Aberystwyth*

YES
people who won't quite say:
Yetman, Yesnaby
people you would like to say:
Low Ardwello

YES, meaning no: *Yesnaby*

YOUTH
crap about jobs done during:
Pulverbatch
resentment of unfairly
apportioned: *Trunch*

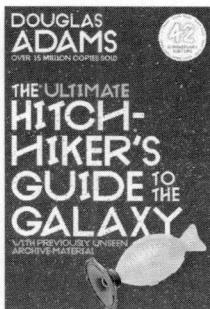

'A thumping good detective-ghost-
horror-whodunit-time travel-romantic-
musical-comedy-epic'

DOUGLAS ADAMS

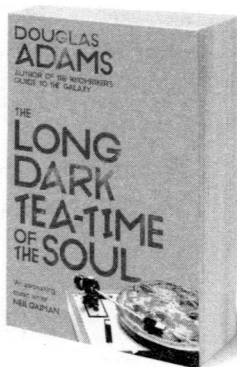

Dirk Gently's Holistic Detective Agency and
The Long Dark Tea-Time of the Soul by Douglas
Adams, author of *The Hitchhiker's Guide to the
Galaxy*, are much-loved cult classics that have
spawned radio dramas, television, theatre and comic
book adaptations across the globe. These new
audio editions are hilariously narrated by Stephen
Mangan – star of *Green Wing*, *Episodes*, and the
original *Dirk Gently* series on the BBC.

AVAILABLE NOW IN PAPERBACK, EBOOK AND AUDIO DOWNLOAD

DOUGLAS ADAMS

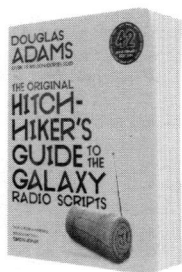

THE ORIGINAL HITCHHIKER'S GUIDE TO THE GALAXY RADIO SCRIPTS

March 1978 saw the first ever transmission of Douglas Adams's *The Hitchhiker's Guide to the Galaxy* on BBC Radio 4; the beginning of a cult phenomenon.

March 2020 marked the 42nd anniversary of that first transmission – 42 being the answer, of course, to the Ultimate Question of Life, the Universe and Everything. To mark the occasion, Pan Macmillan have brought back into print *The Hitchhiker's Guide to the Galaxy: The Original Radio Scripts* with an introduction from Simon Jones.

The collection also includes the previously 'lost' Hitchhiker script from the 25th anniversary edition, 'Sheila's Ear', and the original introductions by producer Geoffrey Perkins and Douglas Adams.

This collection, which is a faithful reproduction of the text as it was first published in 1985, features all twelve original radio scripts – Hitchhiker as it was written and exactly as it was broadcast for the very first time. They include amendments and additions made during recordings and original notes on the writing and producing of the series by Douglas Adams and Geoffrey Perkins. For those who have always loved Douglas Adams, as well as for his new generation of fans, these scripts are essential reading and a must-have piece of Adams memorabilia.